How to TALK Your Way to a BETTER JOB

How to TALK

Your Way to a BETTER JOB

Rosalie H. Smith

MONARCH PRESS

Copyright © 1981 by Rosalie Haiblum Smith
All rights reserved
including the right of reproduction
in whole or in part in any form
Published by MONARCH PRESS
A Simon & Schuster Division of Gulf & Western Corporation
Simon & Schuster Building
1230 Avenue of the Americas
New York, New York 10020

MONARCH PRESS and colophon are trademarks of Simon & Schuster,
registered in the U.S. Patent and Trademark Office.
Designed by Irving Perkins Associates

Manufactured in the United States of America
10 9 8 7 6 5 4 3 2 1
Library of Congress Catalog Card Number: 81-82173

ISBN: 0-671-41880-7

Acknowledgments

WARMEST appreciation to my family that communicates: to Jay for his understanding and encouragement; to Ira, Andria, and Eric for their assistance with editing and typing and for their helpful criticism; to the many friends, colleagues, and students who told me, "You can do it!"

Contents

	INTRODUCTION	1
One	IT WILL WORK FOR YOU	5
Two	STRENGTHENING YOUR IMAGE	11
Three	COMMUNICATE WHEN YOU TALK	23
Four	TALKING IS LIVING	35
Five	YOUR BODY TALKS	45
Six	ARTICULATE	59
Seven	TRY VARIETY TO SPICE UP YOUR VOICE	67
Eight	LOUDER NOT BETTER	77
Nine	SAYING WHAT YOU MEAN	87
Ten	MAKE YOUR WORDS COUNT	93
Eleven	ARE YOU LISTENING?	101
Twelve	MAKING EFFECTIVE PRESENTATIONS TO SMALL AND LARGE GROUPS	107
Thirteen	INTERVIEW IDEAS	125
Fourteen	EFFECTIVE COMMUNICATION SKILLS FOR WOMEN	135
Fifteen	I SHALL BECAUSE I WANT TO	143
	CONCLUSION	151

Introduction

THIS book of skills to help you land a job or move on to a better position was written in response to requests by scores of participants in the seminars and classes I have taught over the last decade. There are countless texts for communication or speech specialists but relatively few guides for businesspeople who want to succeed in their work.

Having been urged to write what I teach in one-day or full-week workshops, or in training sessions in academic settings or at international corporate headquarters, I decided to give the written word number one priority and spent the summer of 1980 writing rather than lecturing and teaching. The contents of this book are based on my course entitled "Oral Communications for Business and Industry."

Individual chapters highlight:

- general communication theory, specifically as it applies to the world of work

- verbal and nonverbal images and messages that you present through your words, voice, appearance, movement, and dress
- speech patterns—articulation, dialects, pronunciation
- language—vocabulary, grammar, fluency
- interview know-how
- presentations to small groups and platform skills—content, delivery, answering questions
- effective communication for women
- exercises to improve vocal quality, pitch, rate, and volume
- quizzes to evaluate abilities and assess needs
- guidelines for assertive, positive communication

How you come across to others and how you view yourself is the underlying theme of this book. That you can begin to switch gears, so to speak, by understanding your strengths and weaknesses in the way you send and receive messages, is the challenge and goal. My aim is to encourage you to see and hear yourself as others do, so that you can develop an objectivity about your own communication skills.

Your image—who you are, what you want to accomplish, where you hope to work, and why you have set your goals in a given direction—will be analyzed, as well as the role of both the voice and body in communication.

I invite you to do some soul-searching and, to add an extra dimension, to try some fantasizing. Mentally form a picture of yourself now and another of the person you would like to be.

Begin by conjuring up, in your mind's eye, who you think you are. Write a list or a paragraph on how you view yourself. After examining yourself, make a list of traits you would like to have, and then develop a character sketch of the person you would like to be. It will be helpful to refer to this self-study as you progress through the book. You will find that you are better able to judge your strengths and weaknesses as you learn more about voice and body language and start to interpret feedback from others. This first step of evaluating yourself should help clarify why and what you want to change or improve. Only if you know why you have set a goal can you steer yourself toward achieving it.

The world is made up of leaders, doers, movers, and followers. You can choose whichever role suits you. Your own intellect, talents, and motivation will determine how far you go.

"Man's reach should exceed his grasp...or what's a heaven for?" wrote Robert Browning in the nineteenth century. This philosophy is still true. Though technology has advanced and our way of life has changed considerably, I believe you have to think in that same positive vein. You have to desire and reach out, working toward achieving more than what comes easily.

1 IT WILL WORK FOR YOU

AN engineer from a utility company said, "I've noticed that the more effective communicator is the one who gets the job. It doesn't necessarily mean that he's the more capable person, but somehow he is the person who gets the job. Why does that happen?"

A department manager in a Massachusetts insurance company asked me, "Would you believe that that guy was offered a vice-presidency just on the basis of the presentation he made at the big board meeting? Why, I've been working toward that VP spot for twelve years, and he's only been around for four. What did he do that I didn't?"

"When I try to offer a new idea at a meeting, no one listens. Then, when someone else, particularly a man, repeats the same idea, everyone says, 'Terrific.' Am I doing something wrong?" questioned a systems analyst with a bank's data-processing department.

The president of a public relations firm said to me, "If I hadn't seen myself on videotape, I'd never have believed that it was time for a new image. Now, after your course, a haircut, new clothes, and a new voice pattern, people come up to me and say, 'You should have done that a long time ago.' I stand up taller and really feel good about myself. The feedback is great. Thank you."

Will it work for you? Yes, it will!

As a professional who has achieved success in my field, I cannot ethically promise "success" for every one of you who reads this book. What I can assure you is that you will be able to evaluate and improve your talking skills, and the results should be positive. You do have to be willing to set objectives, make a contract with yourself, and work toward reaching your goals.

Peter Drucker, the recognized expert in the field of management organization, states in his book *People and Performance: The Best of Peter Drucker on Business*, "As an employee you work with and through other people." This implies that your ultimate success as an employee may depend on your ability to deal effectively with other people, presenting your own thoughts and ideas to them so that they will understand you, your concerns and objectives. It is not only the quality of your work that can lead to a new position, but your ability to explain your work to others. The knowledge of a subject and the skill to express yourself well go hand in hand with advancement and recognition.

Everyone Talks—Make It Work for You

Although everyone speaks, not everyone has the ability to communicate well. At least, not yet.

I am beginning with the basic assumption that you are endowed with average or above-average intelligence and desire the education and experience necessary to advance in your work. You may be interested in landing your first job; or you may be directing your efforts toward gaining promotions and upward mobility in your career.

Just by reading this book, you are demonstrating your

desire to move ahead and indicating a willingness to invest the effort and time needed to improve your communication skills. And that is what this book is about: learning communication skills to make you feel more comfortable and be more effective in business, and developing abilities to present a positive image to those in a position to judge you for a new job or for a promotion. You will be perfecting ways to explain a project to your colleagues in such a way that when the time comes to choose the best one for the job, you are the person remembered and selected. You will learn to function with people of different attitudes and backgrounds, and to become more aware of how you may best project yourself competently despite the other individual's salary, status, job level, or degree of sophistication.

My convictions are based on observation and research of thousands of men and women who have participated in the courses, seminars, and training workshops that I conduct. These people, ranging in age from twenty to sixty, include nonemployed and newly employed individuals, as well as longtime employees who have been working for twenty-five years or more.

I am referring to an endless list of executives, managers, secretaries, salespeople, social workers, clergymen, actuaries, underwriters, teachers, personnel counselors, attorneys, accountants, nurses, doctors, dentists, politicians, and students. I have instructed both native-born Americans—some of whom are naturally articulate and speak with fluency, while others have weak vocabularies, poor breathing habits, and distracting mannerisms—and people learning to adapt to English as their second language.

A computer specialist who emigrated from Poland six years ago told me that his co-workers frequently claimed they could not understand his explanations but were embarrassed to ask him to repeat himself because they felt they still would not be able to follow his thoughts due to his accent and mispronunciations. Paul, who was enrolled in a course for supervisors, said he wanted to improve his English so that he could get his ideas across effectively, as he could not maintain his position as manager of a department if his directions were not understood. I prescribed a program that enabled him to correct specific sounds and to improve his vocabulary.

A native of Jamaica, Shelia, who works for an insurance company, said that she was continually asked what foreign language she spoke. People did not believe that she had spoken English since childhood. The English of Jamaicans is, in fact, very different from American English. Shelia embarked on a course of study with me that stressed changing her pronunciation of vowel sounds. Shelia, a highly motivated woman with a strong willingness to work toward improving her communication skills, has helped herself achieve a series of promotions in the two years since we first met when she was enrolled in one of my courses specifically geared to women.

Shelia is just one of many men and women who have emigrated from India, the Caribbean Islands, or even Great Britain, and who have repeatedly expressed the need to speak and perfect the language of the United States. It is unfortunate that Americans are often intolerant of people who speak differently from themselves. In a country as large as ours, where so few people speak foreign languages, it is sometimes taken for granted that everyone will speak the same language. Therefore, dialects or regional speech patterns may hinder comprehension.

Do You Have What It Takes?

You already have the basic ingredients. You have been talking since childhood. You were born with innate intelligence and a natural ability to charm. What, then, has happened to that charisma you possessed as a baby? Where did you lose the spontaneity of speech? Did you become so concerned about pleasing others that you became self-conscious and uncertain about what you said?

Is it possible that somewhere along the way you became

your own enemy? You did not realize what was happening because you were too busy growing up, but you became supercritical of yourself (and not always for the good), so anxious to please others that the real you got lost. If you can begin to think, act, and talk as if you were your own best friend, you can change all that.

To present yourself to others with a strong self-image, you have to begin to think of yourself as "O.K." (The theory is based on Eric Berne's enormously popular work on Transactional Analysis, *Games People Play*.) A positive view of yourself and a positive effort on your part can make the difference in how far you go.

Contract with yourself to communicate effectively.

Evaluate yourself on the chart that follows. This will give you an immediate opportunity to think about how you talk. Judge yourself as honestly as possible. Don't spend more than a few moments on each point but use your immediate reaction in responding. You will have ample time later for careful study and introspection. You will probably find that your self-evaluation changes as you attempt various exercises related to voice techniques, body language, or other areas. Refer back to the chart to remind yourself of where you began. At the conclusion of the book, you will be directed to do further self-study.

SELF-EVALUATION
HOW DO YOU PROJECT YOUR MESSAGE AND IMAGE?
Rate yourself on a scale of 1-5.

Judge your abilities to speak to one person, small groups (3-15 people), and large groups (15 or more people).

1 = weak
2 = poor
3 = adequate
4 = good
5 = excellent

	One-on-One	Small Group	Large Group
Presentation of Information			
1. Voice: rate			
pitch			
quality			
volume			
2. Articulation			
3. Pronunciation			
Eye Contact			
1. Direct appeal to receivers			
2. Use of notes			
Body Language			
1. Gestures			
2. Facial Expressions			
3. Posture			
4. Grooming			
5. Dress			

(Rate each item separately)

Copyright 1980 DynamiComm

2 STRENGTHENING YOUR IMAGE

THE way you look, the way you sound, the picture you present to others, all constitute your image. As you have perhaps considered the expression "What's in a name?" consider now "What's in an image?" How do you feel about your image?

1. Do you put your best foot forward, presenting a positive, competent person?
2. Do you generally try to look and sound your best when you meet new people?
3. Do you present yourself differently with old and new acquaintances?

The ideal responses would be *yes* to questions 1 and 2. If you responded *no* to these two questions, then you should try to understand more about the person you are and the image you create.

Several answers may apply to the third question. There is no perfect response; it is not unusual to behave differently with different people. You may be thinking *yes*, *no*, *maybe*, or *sometimes* as possible answers to question 3. This indicates that we all have images that may vary depending on what we are doing and thinking, and with whom we are interacting.

A logical follow-up question is: How does the image you present correspond to the one you will need for the job you want?

Until now, you may have given little attention to how other people see and hear you. But the way you are viewed by others is of paramount importance in understanding the image you present and the impression you give.

It requires serious self-examination to focus on the way you look and sound. Few people spend time thinking about how they may be coming across to others until circumstances dictate that it is time to take an objective look at themselves. Now is just that time.

In a highly competitive job market, whether you are job-hunting or want to move ahead, you have no time to lose in working on your image. You always need to project your capabilities, competency, sincerity, enthusiasm, and interest. You should look and act the part of the job you want or the position you hold.

If you are facing an annual job appraisal, or have just been through that process, you may have already identified aspects of yourself that you would like to change or improve. To get that promotion or salary increase, you need to project an up-to-date professional image.

YOUR IMAGE IS LINKED TO YOUR PERSONALITY

Your image is a projection of your personality. Your attitudes are conveyed by your posture, your walk, your clothing, your gestures, your voice, your words, your speech pattern. To assess these aspects of your image you need to become objective about yourself. Look directly at yourself in a mirror, or better still, arrange to see yourself on videotape or study recent home movies of yourself. Borrow or buy a cassette recorder and listen to your voice on a recording.

To analyze yourself, complete the following exercise.
Write two headings on a sheet of paper.
(1) My Visual Image   (2) My Vocal Image

Now, list positive (+) and negative (−) factors that you can identify for each area. For example:

My Visual Image

+	−
Neat	Shift weight from one foot to another
Well-dressed	Slouch in seat
Firm handshake	Avoid eye contact
Friendly look	Few gestures
Good posture	

My Vocal Image

+	−
Low pitch	Poor vocabulary
Pleasant quality	Weak sentence structure
Good volume	Rapid speech

What do you like about yourself? By answering this question you will be able to define your strongest and weakest points. In order to eliminate poor habits, you must recognize what you are doing ineffectively and then replace the old patterns with new, effective communication skills.

It sometimes helps to think of a person who has the personality and image you would like for yourself. Study this individual to figure out what gives you a positive feeling about him or her. Decide which traits you might comfortably adopt without feeling as if you were putting on an act.

SET GOALS

In analyzing yourself, think of the impression you would like to make. Set a goal for yourself. Establish a realistic standard. Consider what you can do to create a more professional look and sound. As mentioned above, look at the people around you, particularly those you admire and who hold the position you are shooting for. Listen to the way these people talk, and list the qualities that you feel might be worth copying.

I generally advise participants in my workshops to "try a new style on for size." You might consider changing the type of clothes you are accustomed to wearing. Shop around in the new departments that many large stores have opened for the business/career person.

Men's departments have always carried a good selection of clothes for the businessman, and department stores are now catering to similar needs of women. Take advantage of seasonal sales to get the best value with limited funds.

You should dress for the job you hope to have and not just for the position you are now holding. To be promoted to a new post, you have to project the image of the individual who is currently in the upper echelon. Your clothes and your manner should silently express that you are right for the new role.

Experiment with a suit that is cut differently. Read fashion magazines so that you can recognize whether jacket lapels are the right width or your skirts the right length. Even the *Wall Street Journal* and *Business Week* deal with clothing trends.

Select colors and styles that flatter you. It might be high time to replace some of your favorite but worn shirts, sweaters, ties, or scarves. Use a new tie or scarf to highlight a serviceable but drab tan or gray suit. Perhaps you should try toning down some of your outfits, not coming on so loud and strong. Whatever you select must match both your personality and the new stronger image that you are determined to develop. Consider buying a new blue blazer: many fashion articles and general commentaries suggest that blue is synonymous with power.

IN WHICH DIRECTION SHOULD YOU CHANGE?

Stronger for you may mean projecting a calmer, softer image. If you have been coming on too strongly and if the people around you find you overpowering, it is time for a low-key approach. That may be achieved by changing **your walk**—don't strut; **your posture**—assume a more natural stance with shoulders comfortably back, but chest not thrust forward; **your voice**—stop bellowing; **your words**—avoid lecturing or talking down to your co-workers; **your tone**—sound receptive instead of belittling and critical; **your hair**—get a new cut and styling to achieve a more naturally finished look; **your clothing**—wear bright not brash colors and styles; **your perfume** or **aftershave lotion**—use a subtle aroma, not one that precedes you into the room and bowls people over. Paint a positive, effective image that will encourage old and new acquaintances to think well of you.

An intelligent, sincere look and sound can influence people in your favor. Remember:

The bully does not talk his/her way to a better job;
Too loud in voice, dress, and makeup is too much;
Being abrasive may earn you a little pink slip at the end of the week.

ASSERTIVE COMMUNICATION—IS IT FOR YOU?

Much has already been written about assertiveness. My aim is to help you see the relationship between the way you communicate and the image you present, and the use of assertive behavior. If you are an assertive individual, you take a stand on issues and your voice supports your ideas by being full-bodied, clear in tone, and easily audible. Because you fully believe in your cause, you come prepared with the necessary data or background to present your information with fluency, using varied vocabulary and good grammar, in a well-organized thought pattern. The assertive speaker uses body language that complements the ideas, so that the sound and look present the same message.

Assertiveness suggests that you stand up for your rights by both speech and deed. You explain yourself only insofar as you feel comfortable and certain, and avoid being intimidated by others' comments or apologetic for your actions. However, you must be prepared to accept consequences for your behavior and statements.

At an interview, if you were asked if you have a preference for working in the home office or in the field, you would have to be prepared to back up your choice. For example, you might say that you would welcome the opportunity to become acquainted with the staff throughout the company, and would be pleased to be placed in the field. The words have a positive ring to them, indicating a preference on your part, but also a definite interest and willingness to accept whichever position might finally be offered to you. It is essential to clarify your terms in your own mind, so that what you say becomes a positive, effective, assertive communication.

Examine the faces below:

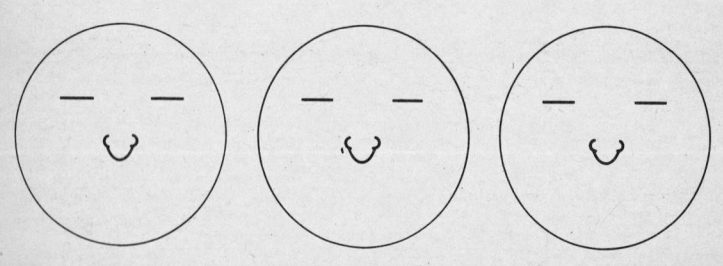

Are they all the same?
Do the eyes all look alike?

Now, look below and answer the same questions. You will find that the identical eyes and noses on the same-shaped faces actually take on definable characteristics by adding to each face a mouth with a different expression to the face. You can now view three types of personalities.

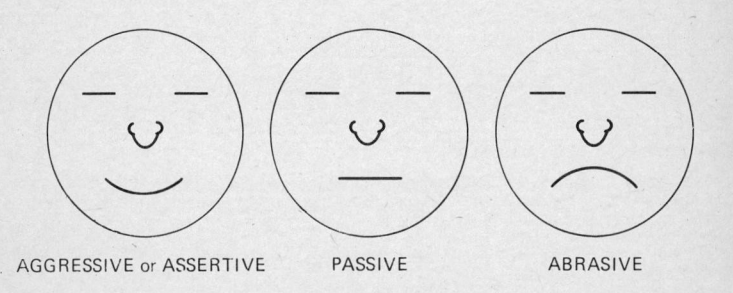

AGGRESSIVE or ASSERTIVE   PASSIVE   ABRASIVE

Some people find the passive individual abrasive as it is quite nerve-racking to be looking for a response, or listening for a comment, and to be faced with silence or a blank look.

You will meet these same faces in Chapter 3 and learn how this behavior affects the environments in which we work.

Are you assertive, aggressive, or abrasive?
Are you passive or nonassertive?
Where do you think you fall on this scale of behavior?

PASSIVE	NONASSERTIVE	ASSERTIVE	AGGRESSIVE	ABRASIVE
1 2 3	4 5	6 7 6	5 4 3	2 1

0 — NEGATIVE COMMUNICATION — POSITIVE COMMUNICATION — NEGATIVE COMMUNICATION — 0

17

Notice that zero lies at either end of the scale. Your chances of influencing someone for your good are nil if you are a passive or abrasive type. To communicate a positive image (+) you need to use assertive communication. Depending on how far you want to go, and the type of position and field you are in, you may need to be more or less aggressive.

Many jobs require a dynamic, creative, go-getter approach. This would bring you to the aggressive part of the scale. That's all right: don't become so involved in terms and labels that you convince yourself "aggressive" means "bad". The numbers on the scale should indicate that extremes are what should be avoided.

To accomplish results and reach your goals, you may need to work with an intensity that has been defined as aggressive. Certainly, most salespeople are expected to act aggressively. Few people at the top of the corporate ladder have gotten there without being aggressive. This explains the rating scale reaching 7, as a high point, and then descending as aggressiveness turns into abrasiveness.

Check the definitions for *assertive* and *aggressive* in your dictionary. You may be surprised at the overlap of synonyms. To *assert* means to state or declare positively and often forcefully or aggressively. One of the synonyms listed for *assertive* is *aggressive*. A bit of a surprise, or are you amazed? This is not what is being taught in assertiveness training courses; note carefully that my stress is on assertive communication.

The most important point, and your prime concern here, is to avoid becoming abrasive. "To abrade" means to cause friction. No one likes friction. We seldom react with pleasure to anything or anyone who rubs us the wrong way. You are not inclined to work with someone whom you find abrasive. The contrary is also true: you will not be the first choice if you are considered abrasive, but will be perceived as a potential problem or a troublemaker. You may claim that you are not abrasive but are playing the role of devil's advocate. My reaction to that is, "You are not the devil's advocate, you are the devil."

The passive or retiring person is easily overlooked. You are the one who tries to get a word in, but finds someone has already made the point. You are the one who does the job (does it very well, too) but the company is reluctant to promote you. What's wrong? You never complain. You never question. And you are never noticed. All around you co-workers tell you what a good egg you are, but they move along and up while you stay stuck and get left behind.

Passive behavior is not low-key but *no*-key.

Can you change? Yes. At the very least you can begin by becoming nonassertive. This will enable you to start thinking about how you can advance to assertive communication. You will be moving from the weak, silent image that you have accepted for yourself until now.

How can you change? You have to look at yourself honestly and determine to make changes in your image. That's the first giant step.

Once you decide that you are not satisfied with the way you are coming across, you will be on your way to coming up with new habits that can replace the old, weak ones. Keep in mind, however, that habits do not go away by wishful thinking. You must break an existing pattern by instituting a new one. Develop assertive skills in place of nonassertive or passive ones. Instead of saying, "I don't know" or "I don't care," take a position. Try, "Yes, lunch from eleven-thirty to twelve-thirty will be fine. Thank you." Study Chapters 5 and 7 to learn more about your verbal and nonverbal language and mannerisms.

What will the result be? Success! Like the little engine that could, in the children's story, you just have to begin to believe, "Yes, I Can."

If you have been wondering where you belong on the scale or which face you wear—passive, nonassertive, assertive, aggressive, or abrasive—then take the quiz "How Do You Communicate?" and discover yourself.

HOW DO YOU COMMUNICATE?

Evaluate your image and how you come across.

Circle the appropriate response(s). Try to be objective and candid. If several of the answers apply, circle each of them. Give your first reaction to each question but attempt to think of specific incidents or experiences that affect your communication.

1. I would rate myself as a (a) strong (b) adequate (c) weak communicator.
2. Others view me as a (a) strong (b) adequate (c) weak communicator.
3. I respond positively to women at meetings who are (a) strong (b) adequate (c) weak communicators.
4. I respond negatively to women at meetings who are (a) strong (b) adequate (c) weak communicators.
5. At meetings, I (a) always (b) generally (c) sometimes (d) almost never (e) never participate in discussions.
6. When I have a response to a question addressed to a group of 2–5 people, I (a) always (b) generally (c) sometimes (d) almost never (e) never give the answer to the question asked.
7. When I have a response to a question addressed to a group of 10 or more, I (a) always (b) generally (c) sometimes (d) almost never (e) never participate in discussions.
8. I consider myself a (a) strong (b) adequate (c) weak listener.
9. When I am part of a group I (a) look all around at all gathered (b) look directly at the person(s) speaking (c) concentrate on my own notes (d) try to respond to the person(s) speaking.
10. When I speak to a group I (a) look around at all gathered (b) look directly at the leader of the group (c) concentrate on my own notes (d) try to adjust to the audience's reaction.
11. When someone looks at me, the first reaction might be that I am a (a) confident (b) capable (c) casual (d) shy (e) thoughtful person.
12. It is usually (a) easy (b) difficult for my colleagues to know what I'm thinking.
13. I am considered a (a) follower (b) mediator (c) leader (d) devil's advocate.
14. Others think of me as (a) aggressive (b) assertive (c) passive (d) abrasive.
15. I consider myself to be (a) aggressive (b) assertive (c) passive (d) abrasive.
16. My preference would be to work (a) as part of a team (b) with one other person (c) alone.
17. My voice is (a) strong (b) pleasant (c) too loud (d) too soft.
18. I tend to speak (a) slowly (b) hesitantly (c) rapidly (d) at different rates.

19. My manner of speech (words and voice) conveys (a) competency (b) confidence (c) knowledge (d) insecurity.
20. I would rate my vocabulary as (a) strong (b) adequate (c) weak.
21. I would consider my pitch to be (a) unduly high (b) high (c) normal (d) low (e) unusually low.
22. My body language is (a) strong (b) adequate (c) weak.
23. My nonverbal language projects (a) confidence (b) defensiveness (c) vulnerability (d) alertness (e) empathy.
24. My facial expressions are (a) always (b) generally (c) sometimes (d) almost never (e) never misunderstood.
25. I'd rate my gestures as (a) strong (b) adequate (c) weak.
26. At meetings I (a) always (b) generally (c) sometimes (d) almost never (e) never present new ideas.
27. When others disagree with me I (a) always (b) generally (c) sometimes (d) almost never (e) never back down.
28. My clothes, makeup and hair-style convey a (a) dynamic (b) casual (c) conservative (d) neglectful image.
29. My voice and body language usually (a) project the same ideas (b) project the same emotion (c) conflict with each other.
30. My words, gestures, and tone convey (a) enthusiasm (b) intelligence (c) credibility (d) insecurity (e) nothing in particular.

To determine your score, multiply each (a) by 5, each (b) by 4, each (c) by 3, each (d) by 2, and each (e) by 1.

If you had several responses to a question, count only the highest letter score. That is, if you responded (a) and (b) to a single question (since instructions direct you to list as many answers as might apply), you would count 5 points toward your total score.

Tally all your points and match your total to the following:

Under 100 points—you tend to be *passive*
100–115 points—you tend to be *abrasive*
116–125 points—you tend to be *assertive*
126 and above—you tend to be *aggressive*

3 COMMUNICATE WHEN YOU TALK

WHEN you talk, do you communicate?

For the purposes of this book, the word *talk* is interchangeable with the word *communicate*. Among the synonyms for *talk* listed in *Webster's New Twentieth Unabridged Dictionary*, you will find *communication*. The stated definition for *communicate* is, "to share; to participate; to have a connection or passage from one to another; said of things, and generally followed by with; to have or hold intercourse or interchange of thoughts; to give or take and receive information, signals, or messages in any way, as by talk, gestures, writing, etc."

To talk your way to success in job-hunting, you have to use your voice and body in an effective manner to send your ideas or messages. You require voice for the production of sounds to say the words you choose. You need your body to add emphasis to these words in a visual and kinesthetic sense. Your ability to write well if you also speak well will add to your credibility.

How you talk with your voice and body conveys a message in itself. The image you give to the receiver may determine whether you get a job, how you progress in a job, and whether you hold on to the job. The way you move, the way you walk, the way you appear, the way you talk and use your words, phrases, expressions, sentence structure, and ideas are all a part of the way you communicate.

Researchers say that as much as 70–90 percent of your day may be spent in some form of communication, depending on your job and the level of your business position. Middle- and upper-management personnel talk and listen throughout their day. Teachers and secretaries spend most of their day communicating messages orally or in writing. Salespersons spend the greater part of their day in communication with others. You are communicating every time you deal with people, each moment that you send or receive a message or exchange an idea.

The business setting includes:

Department meeting
Interview
Casual encounter in the hallway
Meeting in an office
Small or large luncheon meeting
One-on-one report session
Meeting in the parking lot
Training session
Selling and purchasing
Giving orders
Asking directions

You communicate with people on different levels. You talk to colleagues in similar positions or in subordinate posts. You speak to and listen to your department head, manager, or boss.

The ladder of communication has three levels: upward, downward, and lateral.

Study the following diagram to familiarize yourself with this concept.

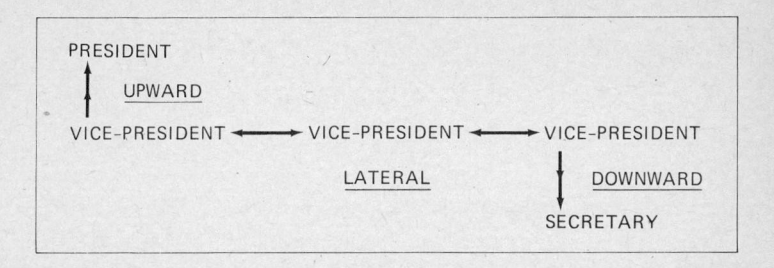

```
PRESIDENT
   ↑
   | UPWARD
VICE-PRESIDENT ←→ VICE-PRESIDENT ←→ VICE-PRESIDENT
                     LATERAL            | DOWNWARD
                                        ↓
                                    SECRETARY
```

The president of a company who speaks to vice-presidents or vice-presidents who speak to their department heads are engaging in downward communication. Downward communication occurs whenever a person in a superior position speaks to a subordinate. A foreman giving instructions to a worker and an executive requesting information from a secretary are also examples of downward communication.

Upward communication involves individuals who hold positions on different steps of the ladder. You are engaging in upward communication when you are interviewed for a job. The supervisor who reports to the department head, who in turn reports to a boss, are both examples of upward communication.

You are taking part in lateral communication when you speak to people on the same level as yourself, your peers.

Your experience in dealing with people will determine how comfortable you are with individuals holding positions up and down the ladder. If you are more accustomed to talking with people who are in similar positions to you—lateral—then you may find it difficult to communicate with individuals who hold a higher rank. It is not unusual for someone to be intimidated by anyone regarded as a boss.

The more contact you have with businesspeople in different situations, the more capable and effective you will be when you talk.

Anytime you are talking with one or more persons to share ideas, understand each other, speak, listen, look, receive or exchange words, and read feedback, you are participating in communication that includes verbal and nonverbal symbols.

Let's look at some examples of effective communication. You are placing a call to arrange an interview and upon hearing the receptionist's greeting, "Mr. Hudd's office," you would say, "Good morning, this is Rosalie Smith calling. Would it be possible to speak with Mr. Hudd?" The receptionist may respond, "May I ask what this call is in reference to?" and your answer might be, "Certainly, I'm interested in setting up an appointment with him. Perhaps you can help me." This exchange gives the secretary a sense of importance because you suggest that she can be of assistance and you are direct in answering her queries. You are observing the rules of common courtesy.

Compare the above dialogue to the following one:

"Mr. Hudd's office."
"Hello, I want to talk to Mr. Hudd."
"May I ask what this call is in reference to?"
"Look, I just want to talk to Mr. Hudd. Is he there or not?"
"I'm sorry I can't tell you anything if you won't answer me."

You can see that you are not progressing in a positive direction. Use appropriate communication to produce a wholesome response from your listener. If you become antagonistic, your receiver will respond in kind. Avoid putting someone on the defensive, whether it is the receiver of your messages or yourself.

Most people have a tendency to react in what psychiatrists call a mirror image. When you become hostile, so does the one to whom you are addressing your remarks. A pleasant statement is more likely than an angry comment to produce another pleasant remark. It may not always be tit for tat, but it should be sincere and cordial. Your aim should be to practice and perfect effective communication. Talk in the suggested ways with friends and relatives. Notice the trust and credibility you will gain. It *can* work.

Your goal should be to have positive interaction with those around you and to achieve a complete understanding of the thoughts, feelings, or needs expressed by both the sender and receiver.

Effective communication implies a willingness as well as a desire to get a message across. It requires one person to send a message and at least one other to receive it. The process requires an attitude of confidence, openness, and cooperation, a spirit of give and take. You, as a thinking individual, unlike an animal, have the power to develop symbols and signals that serve to get your ideas across in an accurate, sophisticated manner.

THE COMMUNICATION PROCESS

True communication takes place when the roles of sender of message and receiver of message are interchanged. You function as the listener at one moment and switch to become the speaker the next, as you are motivated to respond.

Your reaction is the necessary feedback for the communication process to continue.

SENDER	MESSAGE	RECEIVER

What is happening?

A brainstorm, symbolized by a light bulb as in the comics, goes off in your head as you formulate an idea. Simultaneously you select words that will be comprehensible to the person(s) facing you, or to the listener on the other end of the telephone. You use your ability to think and to encode—formulate the symbols or words which make up your written or spoken language.

You are self-motivated, reacting to your own urge to express yourself. At that moment, it is worth reaching out to make your thoughts or feelings understood. This suggests that you should be fully certain of what you want to get across before you open your mouth to articulate words. It is difficult if not impossible to send a message which you have not fully developed. Keep in mind that whatever you encode must eventually be deciphered by the receiver.

To be certain you know what you plan to say, answer the following:

1. *What* do I want to say?
2. *Why* do I want to get this message across?
3. *To whom* am I conveying my idea?
4. *Where* is this exchange taking place?
5. *Which* approach will work best for this subject?
6. *How* brief and accurate can I be?

The points above are no different from those any good news reporter would consider to get a story out.

Make it a regular practice to mentally go through this checklist when you are especially anxious to say what you mean. This list will help the person who says, "I am frequently at a loss for words." It will help any one of you who wonders why you become so nervous that your face becomes flushed, your mouth dry, and your palms sweaty. This formula of running through what, why, to whom, where, which, and how will work. It will enable you to be sure that what you think you want to say is what you finally express.

If you understand and believe in the message you are trying to send it will be worth taking the extra time to quickly cover these points. In the long run, you will save time because it will help you get the job done or it will help you land that first job.

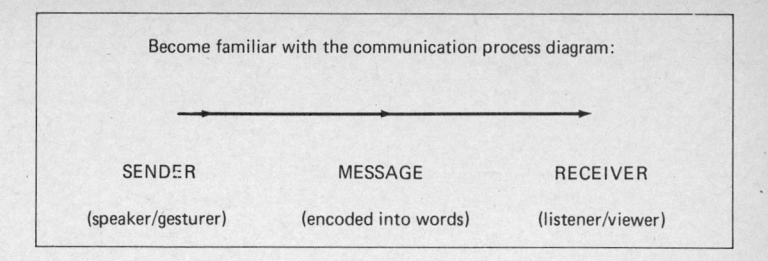

> Become familiar with the communication process diagram:
>
> SENDER → MESSAGE → RECEIVER
> (speaker/gesturer)　(encoded into words)　(listener/viewer)

The next step in the communication process is taken when the receiver becomes the sender. The person(s) on the listening and/or looking end must be in a responsive, receptive state to the message and to the sender. This will allow the receiver to make an honest attempt to comprehend the original message forwarded.

The process of decoding now takes place.

Decoding is the act of analyzing the symbols and translating them into words and thoughts that the listener perceives as comprehensible. The more similar your background is to your partner in communication, the more likely you will achieve understanding. The more you have in common—education, experience, cultural background, age, sex, native language—the greater chances you will have for mutual comprehension of the thoughts being exchanged.

The interaction of talking should result in a circular type of response which will produce feedback. The pattern of sending and receiving now becomes the switch in roles as shown in the diagram below.

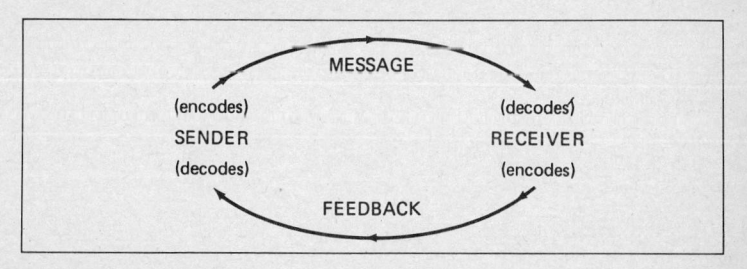

> MESSAGE →
> (encodes)　　　　　(decodes)
> SENDER　　　　　RECEIVER
> (decodes)　　　　　(encodes)
> ← FEEDBACK

Climates—Hot, Cold, or Lukewarm?

Whether you are the receiver or the sender, your receptivity to someone else is influenced by the prevailing climate. *Climate* refers to the atmosphere or environment in which you find yourself and which may encourage or discourage productive conversation.

Differentiate between the concept of the temperature in the room, too hot or too cold as a result of the heating or cooling system, from the climate of the overall setting.

The scale below, ranging from 1 to 4, identifies positive and negative climates. Notice that *cold* at one extreme yields a negative influence, as *overheated* at the other extreme also produces negative interaction.

COLD	COOL	LUKEWARM	COMFORTABLE	HOT	OVERHEATED
1	2	3	4	3	2	1
NEGATIVE			POSITIVE			NEGATIVE

When the prevailing climate is cool or cold, conversation becomes strained and limited. You have certainly heard the phrase "icy stare." If you received that frigid look, you would not be inclined to smile or speak openly and warmly. Likewise, if you are the one who sets up a negative climate by sounding or looking cool, your receivers will respond in a lukewarm or cold manner.

Do you easily become agitated or uptight? Are you the one who gets "hot around the collar"? Negative feelings result from a negative climate. If you tend to overreact to statements, to be too ready to jump in and defend yourself or others when someone makes a simple observation or asks a direct question, then you may be guilty of creating uncomfortable circumstances and a hot or overheated climate.

What type of climate do you think the following remarks will produce?

1. Hi. Wow, do you look tired today! (said sarcastically)
2. O.K., let's cut out the small talk and get down to business. I hate wasting time. (said brusquely)
3. Good morning. Wasn't it great to know the hostages were released today? (said sincerely)
4. Thank you for inviting me in to meet with you this morning. I'm looking forward to learning more about your company. (said warmly)
5. Don't try to sell me on that product. I've tried ten like that before. (said in annoyance)

Your responses were probably: positive climates in statements 3 and 4; negative climates in 1, 2, and 5.

It is not only the wording, obviously, but the tone of voice that will influence the setting.

Situations dictate responses, as you will note in the two columns below.

Positive Climates	Negative Climates
Trusting	Distrustful
Mutual concerns	Conflicting interests
Open mind	Closed mind
Supportive	Defensive
Friendly	Hostile
Democratic	Autocratic
Spontaneous	Formal and rigid

It should appear logical to you that anyone will function more comfortably in a climate that is positive rather than negative. The research of Gibbs, Gibson, Guion, and Weick, psychologists, has extensively explored the area of organizational climates. All the writings emphasize the importance of identifying the atmosphere in which people work. A knowledge of climates will help you clarify how and why you, like most people, communicate more or less effectively in a given environment.

The physical size of the room as well as temperature and furniture placement may also influence climate. You may have heard that colors can make people behave in different ways. It is generally felt that blue is a reassuring color. The presence of blue in an office is associated with a calm atmosphere. Of course, different shades of blue may produce varied feelings. Royal blue would suggest a more dynamic approach than navy blue. But both shades would be perceived as nonthreatening, whereas very bright colors, such as red or Kelly green, might put you on your guard. Your reaction to colors may be totally unconscious. You may not have noticed how the yellow poster made you feel awake and alert. Sunshine yellow tends to perk you up. Brown tones often subdue people. It is said that the earth tones can be comforting. The next time you go into a new room, look around and examine how you react to colors. Does red make you angry? Do you become tense and want to charge ahead as the bull attacks the matador's red cape? Consider the colors of your clothes for the messages they may be communicating. Select furniture or artwork which sets the mood appropriately. Create a climate for positive communication through your use of colors.

A table placed in a corner may seem right for you when you want to get away from your desk and work in privacy. However, the person who is motioned to sit down at that table may feel pushed into a corner. It can produce a cold climate. Similarly, gesturing to the last seat at the end of a table when others are still available, may tell the person he is unimportant.

Make a habit of maintaining a wholesome atmosphere. Wherever negative climates exist, you meet communication barriers.

Communication barriers may result from physical, emotional, or intellectual influences. Your voice and body can play a role in both creating and breaking down such barriers.

Study the three people in this drawing.

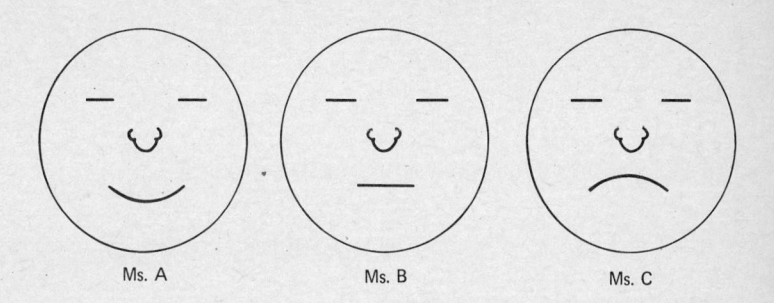

Ms. A   Ms. B   Ms. C

Ms. A is trusting, open, friendly, warm. She transmits a positive (+) image.

Ms. B is defensive, closed, rigid, cool. She transmits a negative (−) image.

Ms. C is hostile, closed, defensive, cold. She transmits a negative (−) image.

Ms. A comes across in a positive way. Her face reflects a willingness to communicate. Not only do the lips smile, but I think you'll agree, the eyes seem to smile. In reality, the eyes are identical for all three faces, as you will readily see if you cover the mouths with a sheet of paper. Notice how the nose and eyes take on a passive or angry cast when you judge them together with the lips that are set either straight or curled down.

Anything negative creates a big zero. Negative communication, negative climates, negative behavior all lead to nothing. As the numbers in red on a balance sheet suggest a negative result, the look and sound of gloom and sadness create a negative interaction.

If you want positive results, a new job, a better explanation, a chance at another position, you will accomplish more if you project a positive feeling to help create a wholesome setting. It helps to think of an old-time saying, "Smile and the world smiles with you."

4 TALKING IS LIVING

TALKING to communicate and communicating to get a message across—what's it all about? What makes men, women, and children talk?

How and why do we talk?

What, in fact, is communication?

What makes some of us good, strong communicators, while others describe themselves as weak, tongue-tied speakers?

What is involved in speaking? I will trace the steps you go through from infancy to childhood to adulthood.

Speech is a learned process. Your environment, your parents, sisters, brothers, cousins, friends, and teachers have all influenced your speech pattern. Does this seem too simple and obvious? Or have you never realized how similarly you speak to your sister or brother?

When was the last time someone said, "You sound just like your father" or "I was sure it was your mother who answered the telephone"? Everyone to whom you have been exposed, beginning in your youth when you were so receptive to adopting others' mannerisms, has influenced you. Most likely, you did not even realize what was taking place.

Does the baby speak? No, but the baby certainly does communicate. He cries when he's hungry or wet or overtired. Baby manages to get Mommy's or Daddy's attention. In fact, the baby even gets action. And that is what communication is all about.

Communication is the sending of a message from one person to another in response to a felt need or desire to share thoughts and/or feelings. This concept was explained in detail in Chapter 3 about the communication process. Our modern-day society is a result of human interaction which has produced increased learning, technology, and socialization. These innovations, in turn, rely upon sophisticated exchanges of information.

Each of us, depending on our intellectual ability, our genes, and our environment, will get messages across differently. Let's return to the baby to understand how talking begins. The baby cries to get attention and the mother picks up the infant and feeds her. Mommy makes soothing sounds and talks to her child. Daddy, too, gets into the act with feeding, changing, and cuddling the baby. This is true in all cultures.

There are over 3,000 different languages spoken throughout the world. All have oral forms, whereas only 25 percent have written forms. It is natural to speak, to create symbols which can serve to exchange our most basic feelings.

Eating, sleeping, breathing, drinking, and thinking are all normal biological functions. So, as the infant is receiving care, the sounds that are being made begin to become familiar. For example, the infant makes sounds that go along with sucking. As the baby licks its lips and smacks them together, the parent will reward the child for voicing "m-m-m-m." Most parents are quickly convinced that their child is saying "Mama" or "Mommy" or "P-p-papa."

The positive response given to the babbling baby encourages more and more sounds which progress to the lalling stage, followed by the formation of one-syllable words. The more encouragement and reinforcement by active conversing in the household, the more responsive and receptive the child will be to speaking, interacting, laughing, playing, and learning.

Some children naturally speak later than others, but we do expect to hear words anytime from nine months to one and one-half years of age. Phrases come next.

"Baby go car. Me play ball. I want now." Are these sentences? Not yet. That comes with the next stage between ages two and three. You can see why it is so important for those taking care of the youngster to practice good speech habits. Remember speech is a learned habit and talking involves imitation and repetition, although it does rely on normal physiological development. The importance of good role models is discussed in Chapter 6 which deals with articulation.

BREATHING FOR SPEECH

Breathing for speech goes hand in hand with breathing for life. Just as each of us should develop good breathing habits to enjoy better health, so should we understand the need to have good breathing habits for effective communication.

The respiratory and digestive systems, together with the brain, are required to produce speech. Thus, you take in air through your nose and mouth while you are speaking and you use that air (breath) for speech.

The process is as follows: The air enters your nose, continues down the back of the mouth to the throat (pharynx), enters the windpipe (trachea), and goes down into the bronchial tubes to fill the lungs which must expand to accept the air. The air you inhale is used for oxygen to supply the needs of your body, as well as the breath for your voice.

The more efficiently you use each breath, the more easily you will be able to speak smoothly.

VIEW OF TRACHEA AND BRONCHIAL TUBES

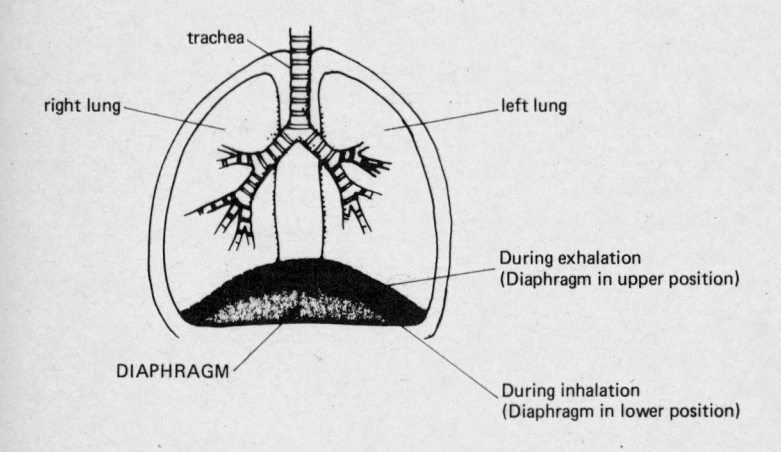

Diagram labels: trachea, right lung, left lung, DIAPHRAGM, During exhalation (Diaphragm in upper position), During inhalation (Diaphragm in lower position)

Note: As you take a breath (inhalation), the diaphragm moves down. As you release the air (exhalation), the diaphragm goes up.

Have you ever observed how a singer uses breath control through use of the chest and abdominal muscles? The lungs are in the chest cavity, surrounded by the rib cage. The chest (thorax) is separated from the abdominal cavity by a muscle called the diaphragm. This muscle moves down, contracting upon inhalation (taking in of air), and compresses the internal organs of the abdomen so that the thoracic cavity increases in size to accommodate the expanded lungs. Meanwhile, the abdominal wall appears to move outward. This is the process you can observe as a singer performs.

Now, look at the diagram on breathing and try to understand the full process of exhalation. Exhalation refers to air leaving through the nose or mouth. The emission of air occurs when the abdominal muscles contract, allowing the internal organs to resume normal position, at the same time that the diaphragm relaxes. Your ability to move the rib cage and the abdominal wall controls the breath stream on which you speak.

SIDE VIEW OF RIB CAGE

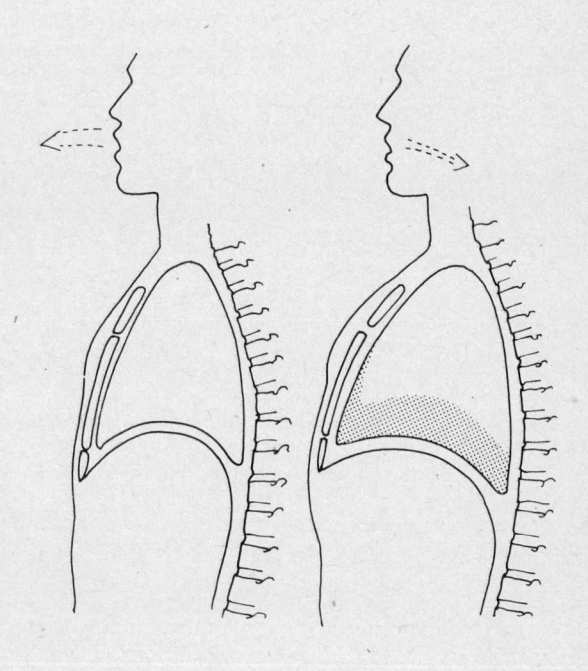

Note: Left drawing shows raised diaphragm and lung at time of exhalation (as air is released). Right drawing shows diaphragm lowered to allow lungs to increase in size during inhalation (as air is taken in).

This has been a very simplified explanation of respiration without mention of the various specific muscles also involved. You can get a clearer picture of how you breathe by watching the natural rise and fall of a sleeping baby's abdomen. Or lie down and place a book on your "stomach," as most laymen refer to the abdomen. You will be able to observe the outward movement of the abdominal wall on the inhalation and as you breathe out for the exhalation, you will see the "belly" relax and move in.

To practice breathing from the diaphragm, which will strengthen your abdominal muscles and increase air intake, stand up and place a lightweight book gently against your abdominal wall. Maintaining a relaxed feeling, but standing up straight, take a deep breath. Hold the breath for a count of three. Exhale. Notice how your "stomach" has moved outward. Be sure you do not allow your shoulders to move up as you inhale. Only the diaphragm and abdomen should be moving to increase the area within the rib cage so that the lungs can expand and take in more air.

Repeat the above steps, but during the exhalation count to three. Say each number aloud slowly and smoothly as you expel the air. Try to develop a comfortable, relaxed attitude while you breathe deeply. Experiment with the above steps, increasing your count to eight or ten if you can build up to an exhalation—airstream—that allows for "*o*ne, tw*o*, thr*ee*, f*ou*r, f*i*ve, s*i*x, s*e*v*e*n, *e*ight, n*i*ne, t*e*n." I have emphasized the vowels because you should try to hold the vowel sound, elongating it more than you normally would.

This is the basic exercise to achieve better control of the pitch, rate, volume, and tone of voice. It is essential that you have breath support if you want to control the nervousness, shortness of breath, or breathiness you may experience while you speak.

LUNGS—TRACHEA—LARYNX—MOUTH—NOSE

Let's go back to the air which is moving up through the windpipe (trachea) from the lungs. From the trachea, the air must pass through the larynx (voice box). The area where the larynx is located is frequently called the Adam's apple, although technically that is the thyroid cartilage that supports the larynx.

The larynx is composed of cartilages that support the muscles controlling this mechanism that may actually hold up the airflow. The vocal folds, also known as the vocal cords, are two folds of tissues within the larynx. The cords or folds contain the muscles needed for the production of voice.

When the vocal folds are at rest, there is a space between them. When the folds move to the midline, closing the vocal tract, the air from the lungs is momentarily blocked. However, once pressure is exerted from below, the air from the lungs pushes the folds apart. The air is then allowed to escape in little puffs. The degree of tension and contraction of the vocal folds together with the air pressure will determine the pitch of your voice, the fundamental frequency, and the intensity of your tone.

Think of your voice in relation to a musical instrument. You may be familiar with the pedals on an organ which are pressed down to fill the bellows with air, and the air reeds in the pipes of the organ which produce sound. Compare, now, the feet pressing on the pedals to the pressure being exerted by the diaphragm on the lungs to force the air out and up through the vocal folds, causing them to vibrate and produce sound.

Have you ever blown air through two blades of grass to show someone how you produce a loud sound? Have you noticed how a guitar is held and how the strings are moved to produce sounds different in both pitch and tone as well as volume? Your voice box, or larynx, relying upon the vocal folds, acts as a musical instrument.

Easy, clear tones are produced by rapid opening and closing of the vocal folds. The better your breath support, and the more pressure exerted upon the folds from the air coming up from the lungs and trachea, the less tension you will develop in the vocal folds. Tension works against smooth and easy vibration for opening and closing of the folds. The folds must be relaxed enough to vibrate with regularity in order to produce a pleasant tone and comfortable pitch. The greater the degree of tension, the higher your pitch will become. As you become tense and muscles tighten in your body, so will the muscles in your neck become taut, including your vocal folds. This is why you may have difficulty producing a low pitch when you become anxious, tense, or angry.

The net result of undue tension is high pitch, poor tonal quality, and weak volume.

To ensure that you have the needed air pressure, you do have to practice good breathing habits. Have you begun jogging? Do you practice aerobic exercises? Are you an advocate of yoga? If you have considered "running for your life," now is the time to decide to "breathe for speaking."

Design a daily schedule for yourself that will include ten to fifteen minutes of breathing time. Use the exercises described earlier in this chapter.

You need good control of a strong, smooth airstream to have good speech. The air which leaves the larynx must pass through the throat (pharynx) in order to enter the mouth or nose. For clear English sounds, the air is emitted ideally through either the nose or mouth, with the majority of sounds requiring oral, not nasal, tones. Most effective speakers will close off the area between the throat and nose, except during the production of the three nasal sounds: m, n, n + g (ng).

The back of the tongue is elevated to the soft palate to effect this closure. Feel this occur as you round your lips and say "oh" as in "oats." Be sure no air is escaping through the nasal passages.

You may have had contact with someone with a cleft palate and may recall the nasal quality of that person's speech. This occurs because the person with a cleft palate is unable, even sometimes after surgery and speech therapy, to fully control the soft palate in order to close off the throat from the nose. Thus, the distortion of sounds, particularly of the vowels which should all be oral tones, becomes most pronounced.

If you have been told that you have a nasal quality, then you are probably allowing air to enter your nose for sounds that should come out of your mouth alone. Bad habits have led you to use an unpleasant, perhaps indistinct, weak voice.

Have you ever associated someone with nasality with the shy, introverted personality? Did you ever wonder if the person who mumbles is afraid to speak clearly because of low self-image? Have you judged someone with lack of clarity in sound as one who also lacks knowledge and "get-up-and-go"?

What happens to the pitch of your own voice as you become nervous and unsure of yourself? It rises, doesn't it? How many times have you wished you had a lower pitch? In Chapter 14, I discuss the negative effect a high pitch may have.

There are exercises in Chapter 14 to help you lower your pitch. You should be cautioned that everyone cannot achieve the same low pitch. The structure of your voice box and vocal folds dictates the optimum pitch for you. However, since you are capable of ranging over two and possibly three octaves, if you match your speaking voice against your singing voice, you can make adjustments within a normal, comfortable range.

It is one thing to recognize your weakness and to bemoan your fate, but the greater accomplishment is in joining the ball game and working your way to home plate.

5 YOUR BODY TALKS

FROM a handshake to a shrug of the shoulders, from an exchange of glances to a sudden gasp in horror or surprise, your body may be speaking louder than your words. Think of being able to decide an issue merely by nodding your head in approval or frowning in rejection. The visual image may be the message that will work for you in your dealings with people at work.

The noted anthropologist and social psychologist Ashley Montagu has explained that the human connection results from the process of communication. People relate to each other via touch, sight, and sound. You are routinely sending signals through:

Facial expressions
Eye contact
Body movement
Posture
Body position, seated or standing
Gestures with hands and/or arms

Kinesics is the study of body language. Speech and language are enhanced by body language. How you move any part of your body, and why, directly influences your interactions with others. Even how closely or how far apart you sit or stand near someone can have impact upon your meeting: *proxemics* is the study of space maintained during communication. Studies are continually being conducted to examine the theory of proxemics in varying cultures; I will explain later how this relates to your behavior.

Would you feel comfortable at work if your chair touched the chair of the person next to you?

When you walk up to someone, do you stand closer than two feet apart as you talk?

Do you shake hands and quickly back off three feet or more?

Your responses to these questions are neither right nor wrong, but indicate how your nonverbal language sends messages to your boss, interviewer, friend, or foe. Your walk, your smile, your squint, your tightly or loosely clasped hands, your shifting feet may help you gain a job or lose one.

First View May Be Last Look

The first view you have of another person is commonly a "checking-out" period. As you might judge a new character in a television sitcom, so you may evaluate anyone who approaches you, particularly for the first time. Just as the actor or actress who is coming onstage is making an entrance, so are you.

Do you make your own entrance with strength? Your look should indicate that you are confident and sincere.

How comfortable are you directing a glance at the person greeting you? The direct look will say, "Here I am, ready to meet and talk with you." No words are necessary if your look is strong.

Do your walk and posture match that message of strong self-image? You need to stand up straight and take comfortable, confident steps. If you are looking down at your feet while walking slowly or hesitantly, your body will not be saying what your voice may be delivering. Your body is projecting "I'm scared and unsure about this meeting," even though you are saying audibly, "Hello, I'm delighted to meet you." Which message do you think will be stronger? A firm handshake, strengthened by momentary eye contact, will reinforce your look of confidence.

How do you sit? On a chair, you say. Of course, but how do you sit on that chair? Do you sit on the edge, lean on one of its arms, clutch the sides, slouch back in the seat; or do you sit up straight (ramrod fashion) so that you appear at attention? An affirmative answer to any one of these poses indicates that you usually tell your audience that you are either an overanxious or supercasual person.

To look alert and interested in the people with whom you are speaking, you need to assume a comfortable, alert posture with your hands in a relaxed position. Your shoulders should be up and partially back, and your chin and head should be held up so that you can maintain eye contact. You should look relaxed, without being totally relaxed. Keep your feet on the floor and do not shake your leg or do a dance while seated.

Drooping shoulders, chin down on neck or chest, eyes half-closed or darting here and there, hands either fidgeting or tightly clasped in your lap clearly proclaim, "I'm afraid"—also shy, worried, unsure, insecure, unprepared, or any of many other negative messages about yourself.

HIGH OR LOW

Do you hold yourself in high esteem? If you do not believe in yourself, why should others? If you do not trust yourself, how can you handle a position of responsibility and trust?

Most of us measure someone else's self-esteem by the height of the shoulders and head. Haughty individuals hold the head up too high, communicating the idea of being above everybody else. Notice how some people five feet four inches tall may give the appearance of being taller, yet others five feet ten inches tall look apologetic and give the impression that they are shorter than they are.

Closing In for Comfort

How close do you get to others? Do you ever wonder if you are too close for comfort?

Most of us are comfortable maintaining a distance of one and one-half to four feet. Sitting or standing closer is generally reserved for intimate situations. In a small group, for example a department meeting, the distance between participants is usually four to twelve feet. A larger room which would allow for distances of twelve feet or more tends to create a public feeling. Many people are uncomfortable when called upon to speak from the front of the room to a large group. I have often heard people say, "I'll give my report from my seat." The speaker is avoiding the public-speaking setting by reducing the distance between himself/ herself and the group.

You have probably not paid much attention to how other people feel about speaking to groups, but you have observed their nervousness. Once you become attuned to watching and listening to others, you will be aware of whether they are at ease standing before others.

Are you confident giving your report when seated in a group of four to seven, but become worried, anxious, and hassled when you are asked to stand and address the gathering? This is a common reaction. Take a new spot once you assume a new position. Forced to stand on your own in front of the group, you change the distance between you and the members of the group, which has become your audience.

You may be worried about your voice carrying. You probably become more tense because you know what you want to say but are uncomfortable because all eyes are now on you. You may want to project your voice, but become especially aware of how you sound and worry that you will be shouting. Still, it is more likely that you are too soft-spoken rather than too loud, so speak out!

CAN OTHERS SENSE YOUR TENSION? PROBABLY ...

You do not have to speak long or say very much for your listeners to know whether you like speaking to them. Your facial expressions and your movements will speak for you and tell how confident you are in your role.

Think of maintaining a smile in reserve at the back of your head, so that your mind can tell you to put it on your face. Repeat the words "relax, relax, relax" as you would use a mantra in Transcendental Meditation. Thinking of smiling or relaxing can be enough to make you release the tensions that work against a smooth delivery or clear thought process.

Become accustomed to placing even weight on both feet. Avoid leaning against a chair or table for support. Sit up and forward, leaning toward the people seated around the table if you are at a group meeting. If the circumstances allow, stand up and take a moment to gather your thoughts as you look around the room as if to say a silent "Hello" to everyone. The adrenaline that charges through your body as you respond to stress can be put to effective use.

Use gestures that require broader movements, rather than tight movements close to the body. Positive gestures come from the shoulder and elbow, not from the wrist. Use both hands to show openness. Avoid standing with arms crossed in front of your chest. Change the weight you are placing on each foot by turning freely to look more directly at people seated to the right or left of you. Don't use this as an opportunity to lean or slouch. Some people cross their feet at the ankles; this is particularly awkward-looking when you are standing in front of even one other person. It confines your own natural movement, as does crossing arms or keeping hands in pockets. You are in a weak position and look hostile or removed.

Convey a look of confidence by using a more dynamic approach in verbal and nonverbal behavior.

Conduct a self-study, examining how you look, how you move, and how you feel about where you sit, stand, and speak. You may already know that you do not like talking to more than three people at once. Or you may be mildly disturbed by small gatherings, but develop sweaty palms, a splotchy rash on your face and neck, and overall discomfort as soon as fifteen or more people are involved. You may have decided at the age of eight that you would never do public speaking. You certainly have that right. It should be helpful, though, for you to understand body language, so that you can interpret others' behavior. In communication, it is as important to know where the other individual is "coming from" as to know what affects you.

Do you move away or back away from people? You may not realize that you move back as someone approaches you, sending the message that you are rejecting that individual or the ideas being expressed.

Some people not only feel comfortable being close to others, but also like to reach out and touch their receivers. You have probably met men (this trait occurs more frequently in males) who poke at you to emphasize points. I know as many men as women who will grab me by the elbow to show a common bond. Sometimes I accept this behavior and at other times I resent it. How do you feel?

You have every reason to choose how you want to react to people who become too close for comfort. Just be aware of what your body is saying as you move back or jump away.

If you are the one doing the "poking" then you should begin to be more respectful of another's space, or "territorial rights"—the area the individual wishes to maintain for himself or herself. Avoid infringing upon someone else's rights; respect differences.

There are cultures that encourage closer contact than ours does. Studies have shown that Americans tend to be "cool" or "aloof," compared to southern Europeans, Latin Americans, and Arabs. You may be perceived as abrasive and pushy by Asians, northern Europeans, Indians, or even other Americans if you attempt to establish too close physical contact with strangers or business acquaintances.

Henry's idea of keeping in touch was offensive. A colleague of his did not know how to cope with Henry's habit of stopping by just to say, "Hi, how are things going?" Jim, who described the scenario to me, is a New Englander, quiet, reserved, a private person. He said that when he had to select a group for a new project design, he found himself wanting to leave Henry out. Henry's ideas and work were excellent. In fact, Jim admitted that it was not the quality of the input but the manner in which Henry worked that had created a conflict. Henry regularly "poked his head in" and Jim wanted to have the benefit of Henry's knowledge without being annoyed by his intrusions.

It seemed clear that Henry was infringing upon Jim's territorial rights. Jim's office was his domain. Henry was unaware of Jim's feelings until Jim realized he had to explain why Henry was not being assigned to the newest project. Jim then took the time and effort to set Henry straight on his too casual, cozy manner. To clear the air and establish better rapport between the two men, Jim had to be willing to openly explain how he was reacting to his colleague's behavior and thus improved an awkward situation to everyone's satisfaction.

Mary, who was raised in England, had just been promoted to office manager in a small manufacturing firm in Connecticut. Her boss asked her to participate in a six-week course for new managers, of which I taught two weeks on communications skills. Mary told me that her greatest difficulty was in giving instructions to her new staff. Her quiet, genteel manner, coupled with an almost inaudible voice, communicated minimal strength as an authority figure. She walked softly, talked softly, all in keeping with her perception of herself as a proper Englishwoman. Cultural influences affect behavior which may work for or against you. Mary explained that she never felt comfortable speaking much above a whisper and therefore liked to deal with everyone on a one-to-one basis, standing quite close to the person.

Mary told me that she sensed her staff found her "too close for their comfort," but she had never considered the simple solution of speaking louder. By speaking up, Mary found that she did not need to be in such close proximity to the men and women with whom she worked. With much effort on her part (Mary had to learn to breathe more efficiently to give her the breath for increased volume), and a change from her usual pattern of approaching others eyeball to eyeball, the communication pattern in Mary's office improved considerably with the result of greater productivity on everyone's part.

THE EYES SPEAK TOO

Do you believe that looks can kill? Can the myths of the "evil eye" be true? Have you ever been warmed by someone's glance? Have you wondered why you find it easy to look some people in the eye, yet avoid direct eye contact with others? Entire books have been written on the language of the eyes alone. In-depth psychological studies have shown the correlation between eye movement and personality. No one likes being stared at, but it would be difficult to prove that everyone likes some eye contact. You can overwhelm a shy person by trying to establish eye contact. You can produce feelings of guilt or discomfort by staring at an individual for an extended period. On the other hand, you can hurt someone's feelings by not making any direct eye contact to indicate your desire to truly reach that person. Here are some general guidelines.

1. Establish immediate, though brief, eye contact when meeting anyone, and on being introduced.
2. Direct your gaze at the person's eyes frequently enough during conversation to indicate you are attentive.
3. When using the name of the person to whom you are speaking, establish momentary eye contact.
4. Avoid closing your eyes, even for a split second, while being addressed.
5. Do not close your eyes or gaze up at the ceiling or down at the floor as you try to decide on your next word or idea.
6. Use a comfortable approach, not an eyeball-to-eyeball stare, as you establish eye contact.
7. Analyze how you feel about eye contact.

You are more likely to feel positive toward people who look at you, rather than away from you. This is a natural reaction. You may discover that you prefer to look at others with short, frequent glances rather than maintain prolonged contact.

Research on eye contact indicates that on the average people look at each other about 60 percent of the time. Some individuals may look continuously, while others look as little as 8 percent of the time. The tendency is to look more while listening than talking, using quick, short glances to watch the speaker. Mutual gaze occurs about one-third of the time people are conversing. A mutual gaze lasts about 1.2 seconds, whereas a glance directed at the speaker lasts about 3 seconds. It is actually difficult to "look someone in the eye," because the visual field goes blank when you attempt to look at the same point for any length of time. The eye of a listener scans the face in rapid, repeated gazes, rather than one steady look. Most people do not like to be stared at, and feel particularly uncomfortable, even threatened, when strangers look one another in the eye. On the other hand, it is presumed to be a friendly look if the persons meeting and talking know each other. Of course, you probably regard a direct look as friendly when you meet a person you know well and enjoy talking to.

Studies have also shown that subject matter, as well as the sex of the speakers, influences the length of time one person looks at another. Have you found yourself looking away when the subject becomes very personal? A discussion of personal topics reduces eye contact.

It is commonly thought that people who are truthful can look you in the eye, and it has been established that those who tell the truth look at others more readily than people who have something to hide. To establish your credibility, you should become comfortable maintaining eye contact. However, avoid any extremes in gazing—too much or too little—which may ultimately create an unfavorable impression.

USE YOUR EYES TO ADVANTAGE

In writing of sexual seduction, Ovid said, "Let your eyes gaze into hers, let the gaze be a confession." Through the ages poets and novelists have praised the "windows of the soul" in recognition of the role eyes play in sending messages.

Use your eyes to the greatest advantage. Think of how you smile. Practice smiling and let your smile shine through your eyes. Look into a mirror and try to smile with your eyes before you move your lips.

Practice looking at others to give good feedback which will keep the conversation moving.

Respond to gazes that indicate mutual interest by returning an equally attentive look.

A woman's eye makeup can enhance and highlight the eyes. Use the eye shadow and mascara discriminatingly, following the advice of professional cosmeticians. Remember, however, that makeup for business should be much more subtle than that for social occasions.

MIXED COMMUNICATIONS—THE BODY SAYS ONE THING, THE WORDS SAY ANOTHER

Your words may send one message while your body language sends another. It is not uncommon for people to be unaware of the conflicting signals they are sending. The listener is thus the recipient of mixed communication, which creates a dilemma: which should you believe, the words or the look?

Should the words be accepted at face value, or should the facial expression that says "I don't believe a word I'm saying" be accepted? Mixed communication confuses the listener and results in contradictory feedback when the reversal of roles from receiver to sender does not occur naturally.

Examine the following situation to understand the way mixed communication occurs. Tom arrives for his appointment at the employment agency dressed in a suit and tie. He wants to apply for summer office work and is trying to look the part—a sensible, realistic approach. The receptionist, Sally, greets Tom, giving him a careful once-over from head to foot. Her look seems to be saying, "What do you think you're all dressed up for?" When Tom asks if office work is available, Sally says (with a toothy grin), "Oh, sure, we get daily calls from a lot of the companies." Jim hears the words, but wonders if the facial expression is not the message he should believe. The look on Sally's face seems to suggest he has come to the wrong place. Tom becomes baffled as to his next move. Should he stand his ground for the job he hopes for, or should he inquire about factory work? He feels confused, and communication between Sally and Tom falters. Sally does not often see such well-dressed young men, even when college students are job-hunting, and without realizing what she is doing, she delivers a message. Her reaction is involuntary.

Remember that communication is multiphasic. You use all your senses to talk. This means that you are continually sending messages via your sense of hearing, sight, touch, smell, and feel. You rely equally upon your senses to receive.

It may be easy for you to equate receiving the message with how you act when you see a flashing red light at an intersection.

> You *stop* (come to a halt bodily).
> You *look* (observe all around with care).
> You *listen* (attend to any sounds which should be heeded).

Only after you *stop, look*, and *listen* do you move on.

Verbal and nonverbal language is routinely being influenced both intentionally and unintentionally by our senses.

FACE-TO-FACE ENCOUNTERS REINFORCE COMMUNICATION

It is logical that the face-to-face encounter provides the best setting for effective communication. In a face-to-face position, you can truly put your senses into full play. Eye contact can only be established if you are facing each other. Reaching out to shake another's hand, or to receive a hand, can only occur if you are face to face. Pulling away, pushing your chair back to indicate you are ready to leave, is only evident if you are seated face to face.

Face-to-face settings allow for the most interaction. They encourage input on the part of the two or more persons sitting, speaking, or working together.

Examine how well you make use of your senses in daily conversations. How well do you use your senses at interviews or at casual meetings in the parking lot or at the coffee machine? How effectively do you make your body work for you at a department meeting or in a training session?

Make a list of what you observe about other people's body language, as well as your own. Keep a separate sheet for nonverbal language that has contributed to better understanding and another sheet for nonverbal language that led to less understanding or ineffective communication.

Keep a diary, indicating the day, situation, and action involved to determine how certain nonverbal language influences the outcome of your business transactions. Remember to make a point of noticing the strengths of people whom you admire and try to emulate their strong, firm gestures, their well-positioned feet, their animated expressions, and their overall carriage.

Observe and practice body language that conveys competency. Apply this saying by Confucius: "When you have faults, do not fear to abandon them."

6 ARTICULATE

THE training director of an insurance company asked me to help one of her employees. This was an unusual situation that would require private work with a twenty-six-year-old man whose speech pattern was holding him back from promotions. I had been selected to work with him because of my background in speech pathology and my familiarity with problems of dialect speech. Harry T. grew up in a New York black community, attended a private high school, and continued on to college and then graduate school in New England. He received his master's in business administration, was employed immediately, and was quickly recognized as a man who could do the job but could not communicate his abilities.

Harry was a highly motivated man who had set clear goals for himself. He actually interviewed me to determine whether or not my approach for altering his speech pattern could achieve the results he wanted. Our agreement that

59

"Black English" was all right for his personal world but unacceptable in the corporate community allowed for setting up a program of lessons in successful communication that led to the promotion Harry and his company wanted.

What were some of his problems? He spoke very softly, frequently dropping almost to inaudibility at the ends of sentences. Harry generally shortened all words ending in *ing* to *in*. For example, "go*ing*" became "go*in*," "runn*ing*" was "runn*in*." Harry's speech was characterized by a slurring of words. He also reversed the sounds in *ask*, saying *ax*. His grammar was proper, for the most part; however, he substituted *don't* for *doesn't*. Had Harry identified these patterns? No, not until we began work with a tape recorder and then he resolved to pay greater attention to his speech.

How, you may wonder, does someone retain the "ghetto speech" of his youth, after being well educated and exposed to other people in other communities? The answer is simple: we are the product of our environments, as explained in Chapter 4. No environment or culture is better than another, but the speech pattern you learn in childhood is the one you tend to practice unless a concerted effort is made to change it. Therefore, since you learn to talk by imitation, repetition, and habit, in order to develop what might be regarded as educated, literate American English, you would need an early exposure to the sounds that you would be incorporating into your everyday adult speech.

As discussed in the first chapters of the book, the patterns learned in your formative years are continually reinforced by family, friends, and teachers. As long as you remain a part of the original culture, no changes in speech habits may be necessary. Think back to the immigrant families of the turn of the century. Some parents spoke no English, or more frequently, they spoke English with a foreign accent. Their children had to make a conscious effort to improve their own speech. As they left the home community and ventured into the outside business world, they discovered that they spoke differently and some people had trouble understanding them. Problems arose because they were in a new setting.

Let me quickly retrace the way a child begins to learn sounds. At first, a baby only cries to deliver the message "I'm hungry, I'm wet, I'm uncomfortable." This is a cry for help. When the parent responds in soft, tender tones and words to calm the infant, the infant becomes accustomed to hearing certain sounds, feels good about being handled, likes the tender, loving care, and associates his cry with a pleasant response. As the thought processes develop, the child has greater comprehension of the surroundings and learns how to communicate with the environment.

Words with easily repeated sounds are the first words repeated by the infant. The child is mimicking those around him. If the parent uses full sentences, and if others also encourage repetition of grammatically correct sentences, then by the age of two or three, the youngster may be capable of saying, "I want to go for a ride. The car is fun." The child is using full sentences in imitation of what has been heard.

What you do not hear, you cannot mimic.

This is, of course, the problem with the hard-of-hearing or deaf person. The learned process of speech only occurs if the normal hearing and constant repetition of the new sounds and words become meaningful; partial or complete deprivation of sound hinders normal language development. A baby who hears only baby talk, or one who is in a hectic, harried household where people do not take the time to speak in full sentences, might at the age of three, four, or five still be saying, "Me go ride."

A child will assume words are pronounced as they are spoken by those from whom he/she has learned. Depending on the pronunciation that a child is exposed to, the child will say "chile" or "child," "tole" or "told," "chillun" or "children," "aks" or "ask." The omission of the final *d* sound sometimes occurs in black dialect speech, as does the reversal of some consonants. If the child is not exposed to other speech patterns and encouraged to change articulation, the old habits of pronunciation continue into adulthood.

How important is all of this? Only you can make an honest assessment. It becomes more important as you set out to find a job and sense that the way you are saying words is getting in the way of proper reception. You are perhaps misunderstood. You are even judged to be less intelligent or less educated, merely because you say sounds and words differently.

You can move along, and perhaps get a good job if you stay within your original community. Once you venture out into the city or into the larger business community, you will probably be expected to use standard speech.

What is standard speech? For the different sections of our country, we have what is commonly referred to as General American, Eastern, and Southern Standard speech. It is the pattern practiced by the so-called literate, educated members of our society. The speech that you hear used by television or radio announcers, and most specifically by national news commentators like Dan Rather, Walter Cronkite, or Jessica Savitch, is standard.

It can be argued that dialect speech is fine and that holding on to one's heritage should be encouraged. However, it can also be argued, "When in Rome, do as the Romans do." If you want to talk yourself to a better job, then you will have to convey your ideas clearly and easily. You are going to have to sound your best, and your best is that which is most effective for your listener. You achieve nothing by distracting your listener from what you are saying by using a speech pattern that is different from what is commonly accepted and expected. The job you want and the company you want to work for have an established image that you are expected to match and maintain. This is especially true of large firms that have branches all over the United States and the world. The interviewer will listen to you and decide whether you will sound right in the position to be filled. The way you talk should add to your credibility, not detract from your ability.

Check your own articulation. Recording your reading, say each of the following words aloud. Read the list through to familiarize yourself with it. Say the number first and then say the word. Do not try to speak differently from the normal conversational manner you use.

1. pineapple
2. beat
3. means
4. we
5. which
6. freedom
7. having
8. if
9. think
10. tentative
11. danger
12. no
13. little
14. red
15. arrow
16. seize
17. zoology
18. shout
19. measure
20. youth
21. human
22. coil
23. going
24. hanging

Play the recording and listen carefully to how you say the numbers and each word. Is your pronunciation clear?

Use each word in a sentence and record yourself again.

CHECK LIST OF SPEECH HABITS

1. Do you articulate clearly and distinctly?
2. Are your vowel sounds too prolonged?
3. Are your vowel sounds insufficiently prolonged?
4. Do you run one word into another?
5. Do you tend to drop endings of words?
6. Do others frequently ask you to repeat yourself?
7. Do you add sounds that do not belong?
8. Do you reverse sounds in words? (e.g., *pattern*, not *pat-tren*)
9. Are there certain sounds that are difficult to say?
10. Are you frequently uncertain about the pronunciation of some sounds and/or words?

If you answered *yes* or *maybe* to numbers 2 through 10, then you should devote at least a half hour weekly to practicing the sounds and lists of words and sentences below. Set a schedule for yourself, allocating a minimum of ten minutes at least three times a week. Work with a tape recorder or cassette player and use a mirror to check the placement of your lips, tongue, and teeth for the sounds. Keep a daily diary to record the time spent and sounds practiced.

In the list that follows you will find key words for drill. Repeat each word three to five times and use each in a short sentence. Then read the accompanying sentence to see how you should use the indicated sound in a word and sentence. Record and play back.

PRACTICE WORDS AND SENTENCES

The words are examples of the consonant and vowel sounds you should be saying distinctly. Consonant sounds are often in pairs, e.g., *p* and *b*—the *p* is voiceless, the *b* is voiced.

A voiced sound requires vibration of the vocal folds. Place your fingers lightly on the Adam's apple and feel the slight movement as you say the *b* or *d* or *m*.

Voiceless sounds result from the emitting of air. To understand this, blow breath out and say *p* or *t* or *k*.

Sound	Word	Sentence
p	pen, happy, up	Philip Piper introduced a new sales pitch.
b	boy, maybe, sub	Viewers of the Super Bowl agreed both teams had cause to celebrate.
m	most, climber, am	Mary Martin's son has climbed to the top of stardom, playing J.R. on *Dallas*.
wh	what, anywhere	What you say and to whom you say it will count for or against you.

Sound	Word	Sentence
w	watch, away	"Waste not, want not" is a phrase associated with the twenties and thirties.
t	top, butter, cat	A common goal for many now is to try to reach the top of the corporate ladder.
d	do, adding, fad	Dan Addison called the meeting for Tuesday at noon.
n	no, owner, nine	None of the necessary papers was filed on time.
l	look, also, call	Lawrence Hall called the personnel manager.
r	run, very, car	New York, Connecticut, and Rhode Island all run lotteries.
s	say, myself, us	Some say nothing succeeds like success.
z	zipper, lazy, buzz	The office at the zoo called in orders for new computers.
sh	shot, notion, rush	She recognized that the situation would lead to a full shutdown.
zh	division, rouge	Television is an electronic treasure.
ch	chair, matches	Which of the Texas cheerleaders did Mr. Chalmers choose for the beach ad?
dg	giant, enjoy, edge	The engineering firm was awarded the giant bridge contract.
j	you, junior	You are the youngest junior officer in that particular bank.
k	cow, turkey, bike	How awake are company executives at a breakfast meeting?
g	go, began, leg	Gary Riggs and Helga Gregory were appointed chairpersons.
ng	finger, thanks, king	Club Med advertised a special week for swinging singles.
f	fun, offer, laugh	Finalize the figures before you present them to Ms. Hoffernam.
v	vie, divide, glove	Dr. Braverman verified the report on her vital signs.

Sound	Word	Sentence
th	think, fourth	Think positive thoughts on your fiftieth birthday.
th	they, neither, with	They would rather delay the project than risk those problems.
h*	how, behind	Howard and Helen Ahern arrived at O'Hare ahead of schedule.

h is sometimes silent at the beginning of words, as in *hourly, honest.*

7 TRY VARIETY TO SPICE UP YOUR VOICE

WHEN I was a freshman faculty adviser at the University of Hartford, I would frequently meet with parents who had phoned me earlier in the semester to discuss their youngsters' problems. Invariably, at the first in-person encounter, several parents would say they were certain their son or daughter was getting the right advice because I sounded so well informed and concerned when we had talked on the telephone. Needless to say, I was pleased to hear these comments.

These parents had placed their trust in me to help the students through the difficult freshman year. In addition to placing their faith in me, they were extending it to the school where I taught. As an assistant professor, I represented the university to them. I was projecting an image for myself, as well as for my employer.

Every time you speak, those for whom or with whom you work are also being evaluated, if only indirectly. Your manager, or your company, or your colleague, may either bask in the glow of your communication successes or find themselves answerable for your deficiencies.

Is your communication positive or negative?
Do you turn people off by the tone of your voice?
Does the tone of your voice work for you or against you?
Do you reach out to others by the way you sound?
Does your voice make others *stop*, *look*, and *listen*?

A quality in your voice should reach out to others, saying, "I want you to listen to me because we have something worth exchanging." Your tone of voice reflects your personality. The listener uses the sound as a barometer to judge your attitudes, interests, likes, and dislikes—even to evaluate your intelligence.

Maybe it is not fair for others to judge you by the way you sound, but the reality is that we all sometimes do. Don't you often judge others by the way they sound?

When You Speak, Do Others Listen?

Why do people listen to that man or woman, and not to me, you ask. Do you send out a message that communicates, "I'm not worth listening to"?

Does the quality of your brainstorm not come across because the quality of your voice says, "I'm not so sure if this idea has any merit"? Do you say whatever it is you want to say breathlessly, gasping for air and becoming inaudible as you reach the end of your statement? If you have been nodding your head to these questions, then you should decide now to improve your voice.

Quality or Quantity?

In these days of dual-career families, it has become commonplace for parents to say that it is not the amount of time they spend with their children that counts, but rather, the kind of contact they have with their sons and daughters. This home situation can be likened to the work setting: it is not how much you talk but how you talk that matters. Continuing with this theory, it is not the amount of communicating you do in your position, but the quality of the communication taking place between you and your superiors, subordinates, or co-workers, that is important.

You must give a priority rating to quality of talking, not quantity. In Chapter 9, you will learn the value of using words that ensure you are saying what you mean to say. Throughout the book I have been stressing the need for you to get your message across; my message to you now is that whatever you want to project must be said with a special quality in your voice that adds to the words you are using.

You must establish your own credibility with your voice. The words you choose—your verbal language—have to be reinforced and complemented by your nonverbal language. Vocal characteristics fall under the category of nonverbal behavior even though the words themselves rely upon the voice. How these words sound is of paramount importance in the way they will be perceived and received.

Voice, like body movement, is a part of your nonverbal language. There are four components of voice which you can adjust and vary. These components are:

1. Quality
2. Pitch
3. Rate
4. Volume

The pitch of one's voice is also discussed in Chapters 4 and 14. You should try to use a pitch that is appropriate for you. As you matured, your voice changed and the pitch probably became lower. This is true for males and females. The man who still sounds like a young boy, or perhaps a girl, is not using the vocal folds to advantage. The woman who is told, "Oh, I thought you were a teenager when we spoke on the phone," has been practicing poor vocal habits, unless her vocal folds are unusually short.

A question almost always ends with a higher pitch. If most of your statements, however, are delivered in a high pitch you may be conveying the idea that you question what you are saying. It is easier and more pleasant to listen to someone with a low pitch.

The person with a very high pitch may frequently suffer from laryngitis and loss of voice following a cold or after a good deal of talking. This results from misuse or abuse of the vocal folds. Good breathing and a relaxed body and state of mind help keep the pitch down. The more tense you are, the more strident your tone, and the scratchier your voice will be. Practice the exercises in Chapters 5 and 6, which deal with breathing and articulation.

If an unduly high-pitched voice can be irritating, does that imply that a low-pitched voice is always good? Yes and no. The lower pitched voice is generally richer in tone and more easily modulated for volume and projection of sound. Sometimes, though, you hear someone with a too low pitch and detect a harsh, hoarse, husky and/or "throaty" tone. You should avoid a pitch at either extreme of the scale.

Pitch is determined by the length, width, or thickness of the folds and their elasticity and tension.

Age and sex differences influence pitch. As you get older there is usually a loss in the higher notes. A soprano often becomes a mezzo-soprano, or a tenor may shift to a baritone.

The female's vocal folds are roughly one-third shorter than the male's and there is generally less muscle, fat, and tissue. The resultant sound is a higher pitch.

The pitch you use most often has been determined by your anatomy, but is influenced greatly by your vocal habits. Therefore, you can make adjustments for the better to produce a pitch which will be more comfortable for you and those listening to you. Everyone has an optimum pitch, the level at which an individual can best produce rich, full, resonant tones.

Try to vary your pitch with your message. Experiment with producing lower or higher tones by recording your reading. It will surprise you to hear how seldom you change pitch or how regularly, in singsong fashion, you rely on the same pitch changes. The inflections you use can strengthen your message. Certain emotional states are associated with specific pitches. Let your voice reflect surprise, questioning, or happiness with a higher tone, whereas sincerity, thoughtfulness, concern, and diligence should be projected with a lower pitch.

Practice saying vowel sounds on different pitch levels. Play a scale on a piano to help you differentiate the different levels you are capable of reaching.

A *full-bodied voice* adds credibility to your words.

A *sincere, warm tone* makes you more believable.

A *clear, dynamic quality* tells your listener you are alert, awake, and set to do the job.

The quality of your voice can communicate your capability as well as your credibility. What do you tell others about yourself when you speak with a whining, nasal sound? What do you convey in a twenty-minute talk delivered in muffled tones? What does an audience think of the speaker whose voice is lifeless? That's right, you've guessed the answer.

You, with the whining, lifeless, nasal, muffled voice, are a complainer (at best), unenthusiastic (for sure), and incompetent (at worst); the image you are projecting is inescapably negative. With such a delivery your words might not be heard, let alone understood, because your audience is turned off. After all, who wants to deal with anyone who sounds bored with himself or his job, or just plain tired of it all?

On a scale of 1 to 10, your voice quality must measure up to a minimum of 5 for you to be an effective speaker.

Use the chart at the end of this chapter to analyze what your voice projects.

Place a cassette recorder near your telephone to catch how you use your voice in phone calls. (Your intention should be to record yourself, not the other party.) Consider how important your voice becomes to the person on the other end of the wire. A phone call is a person-to-person transaction without the benefit of body language. Your words and voice are the sole means of conveying what you think and feel. No other elements play a role.

Do you often meet someone new who says, "Oh, you don't look anything like you sound," or do they say, "I knew you by your voice. You're just the way I imagined you." Both of these statements can be interpreted as complimentary, but the first statement clearly indicates a contradiction in the way you look and sound.

LET YOUR VOICE SMILE

The quality or tone of your voice should correspond to the image you hope to project. If your voice does not sound warm and pleasant on the telephone, the caller may decide you are not a smiling, friendly person. If you sound dull and listless, the caller may further assume you will not follow through with the request at hand because you are not energetic enough to take the initiative. Your voice must convey the idea that you will be agreeable to take the necessary action.

The number of words you use will not necessarily change the impression you are sending. No matter how many times you repeat, "O.K., I'll do that," your lack of animation will not be reassuring. Get to know what you sound like. Watch other people's reactions to you. Identify the tone of voice you like in others. Set goals for yourself.

Listen carefully to the people around you, paying particular attention to those with whom you feel comfortable.

Make a list of adjectives that describe the voices of people you like, respect, and wish to emulate. Concentrate on the sound of television, radio, movie personalities, and start to become aware of how you feel as you listen to them. What is special about the sound of Michael Landon or Gregory Peck or Mary Tyler Moore or Marlo Thomas? Why do so many people find Mike Wallace or Barbara Walters interesting enough to watch and listen to frequently?

Listen to your own voice to determine how others may be reacting to the sound, not the words or your appearance.

WHAT DOES THE QUALITY OF MY VOICE COMMUNICATE?

Use a scale of 1 to 10 to plot your voice.

              1 2 3 4 5 6 7 8 9 10
Competency   _____
Animation   _____
Personability _____
Alertness   _____
Believability _____
Intelligence   _____
Liveliness   _____
Inspiration   _____
Trust   _____
Your true self _____

Reading down the list of characteristics, you may have noticed that the words spell *capability*. *Credibility* and *capability* are what your voice should suggest.

To evaluate yourself further for vocal habits, answer the following:

1. Does the tone of my voice add to my message?
2. Is my pitch pleasing to others?
3. Is my voice hollow, strident, too husky?
4. Do I tend to become nasal sounding?
5. Do I speak inaudibly so that others must strain to hear me?
6. Am I so loud that others find me overpowering?
7. Am I loud enough for comfortable communication?
8. Does my voice lack vitality so that I lose my listener?

Items 1, 2, and 7 should be your only *yes* responses if your quality, pitch, and volume are being used effectively.

The chart below will give you an indication of how you use your voice to project yourself. Try to have your voice reflect the pattern indicated for assertiveness.

VOCAL CHARACTERISTICS THAT INFLUENCE SPEAKERS AND LISTENERS IN THEIR COMMUNICATION ENCOUNTERS

Assertive Pattern	Nonassertive	Abrasive
Volume—moderate to strong (loud), varied	Volume—low to moderate, nonvaried	Volume—unduly low; overly loud; nonvaried
Rate—medium to rapid, varied	Rate—slow (hesitant), nonvaried, singsong	Rate—even and slow; very rapid; singsong
Pitch—medium to low, varied	Pitch—very high; very low, nonvaried	Pitch—unduly high; very low; nonvaried

Assertive Pattern	Nonassertive	Abrasive
Quality—varied tone	Quality—monotone	Quality—monotone
clear (oral)	hollow	highly emotional
vibrant	nasal	overly dramatic
dynamic	denasal	strident
full-bodied	quivering	hoarse; harsh
confident	lifeless	unusually husky
sincere	listless	unconcerned
responsive	childlike	cold
warm	unsure	dull
pleasant	sad	nasal and denasal
intelligent	apologetic	whining
interested	pleading	overly persistent
alert	coy	surly; nasty
		snippy; abrupt

Copyright 1979 DynamiComm

8 LOUDER NOT BETTER

IT does not always follow that he who talks loudest talks last. As in the case of speaking too quickly or too slowly, the extreme use of volume, like the extreme use of rate, will result more often in negative rather than positive, effective communication.

You may be unaware of the level at which you generally speak; on the other hand, you may be quick to admit that people have frequently requested, "Please, speak up," or "Hey, stop yelling at me!"

If you speak too softly, then any idea you have, no matter how innovative, interesting, or entertaining, may very well go unheard and you may miss the perfect opportunity to contribute your expertise or to demonstrate your willingness to do a job, simply because you were seen but not heard.

Whatever you say, state it in a volume which matches the situation and the number of people involved. Consider how far away or close you are to the person(s) listening to you. If the fan or air conditioner is noisy, if there is background noise from an office or factory, if you sense difficulty on the part of your receiver(s), then speak a little louder.

Generally speaking, the larger the size of the group, the louder you must speak. However, you should never be too loud for the comfort of those who are seated closest to you. You should avoid using a volume level that might be better associated with cheering in a stadium.

In order to determine the appropriate volume, you should judge:

the setting (type of room and size)
the role you play in the encounter
the number of people involved
the subject under discussion
the image you wish to project
the atmosphere or climate in the encounter
how well your own voice projects

The last point is important. If you have a naturally low pitch, your voice will probably be more resonant. This means that it will have a strong tone and be audible to most individuals. The higher your pitch, the more likely that you will have a less resonant quality and you will have to increase your volume to be readily heard by others.

If you are talking to someone with a hearing problem, your use of clearer articulation with slightly augmented volume may be of great benefit. Individuals with hearing losses due to nerve damage, however, may actually be irritated by your undue loudness. Check people's eyes to ascertain if they are lipreading, and if you suspect a hearing problem, turn your face more directly to the listener, slow down (within a normal rate range), articulate carefully, and use a volume level which you know carries well. Whenever you cut off the endings of words, or swallow words and phrases, or try to rush through a sentence breathlessly, your volume level will decrease. It is important to have adequate breath control to maintain the strong sound of a full-bodied voice that carries to one or twenty people.

If you have the choice of using a microphone, I strongly urge you to take advantage of this technical amplification. Here again, you will be helping anyone with a hearing loss. You may have noticed that some of your friends or colleagues always insist on sitting "up front," close to the speaker. This is a common pattern for people who are hard-of-hearing and who do not wish to make an issue of their problem, but do want to catch every word. By sitting closer to the speaker, they can watch the face carefully while cutting down on the space through which the sound must carry.

A woman in her late sixties, Vivian H., was attending a seminar in Fort Lauderdale, Florida, that I was conducting. It involved role-playing, as well as lectures and discussion. As a participant in one of the role-play exercises she astounded all the women, with whom she had worked closely in the nonprofit organization sponsoring the seminar, by asking her partner to please turn around and look at her when she spoke since she was hard-of-hearing.

Vivian had been managing to cover her problem until that day. As we talked about communication and how people perceive each other, she explained to me afterward that she no longer wanted anyone to think her senile or absentminded when in reality she was just not fully hearing and understanding what was being said to her.

You need not be sixty years old to have such a problem, nor should you wait for your sixties to unmask your difficulty. I find that everyone in a group is more than willing to accommodate someone with a handicap if the participants are made aware of the situation. You will surely be recognized and thanked for showing consideration to someone who is hard-of-hearing. You will likewise be thanked by the person to whom you own up about your own hearing problems because you will be assuring easier communication.

Hints for using a microphone:

- Check that it is connected and turned on.
- Speak in a natural voice, directing your breath stream toward the microphone.
- Raise or lower the microphone, as indicated by your own height. It should be no higher than mouth level.
- If it is at all possible, test the microphone before the group has gathered. Adjust the volume level and practice speaking into it for a few moments to be sure your voice is carrying well.
- Convince yourself that it will be more helpful to use the microphone and be heard, than to apologize and become flustered over not being audible to everyone.
- Remember that it is a more polished, credible presentation if you stand at a podium and use the microphone. This knowledge in itself should serve as positive reinforcement for calming you down.
- Speak to your audience, not the microphone. Look up and out at the group, not down at your notes.

For those thinking, "I'll never be in front of a group and need to use a microphone, but I need to be louder when I speak to anyone," I offer the following exercises. After reading steps 1, 2, and 3, use a tape recorder or cassette player and say the following words and sentences or phrases:

1. Hello.
2. One, Two, Three, Four, Five.
3. Stop.
4. Stop now. Stop that.
5. I think you're right. I think you're wrong.
6. O.K.

Step one. For your first reading, use what you consider to be your natural volume. Play the reading back before you go on to step 2.

Step two. Read the word(s) on each line in a whisper, and then in a louder voice. Play the recording back and listen carefully to the difference in the volume level, making a mental note of the two degrees of loudness. Be sure they are clearly different.

Step three. Repeat the reading of each line, but this time use the louder voice (probably your normal volume) and then shout each word, sentence, or phrase. Play the recording back and again register the sound of your voice. You will discover, I predict, that what you thought to be shouting will merely be a loud reading. Practice this level of projection.

MAKE YOUR VOWELS REACH ACROSS

The sounds in each of the words in the exercise lend themselves to a clear production of tone. Look back and underline all the vowel sounds. These are the important ones for carrying your voice. Review the exercises on breathing in chapter 4 to help you develop the needed breath support for increasing your volume.

Ask people who know you well and with whom you are comfortable to tell you how they react to the sound of your speaking louder. Make a conscious effort to make your voice *reach across* the table or desk or empty space between you and the other person. In this case, being louder might just be better.

A final exercise, for those who tend to become nervous and speak too softly, is based on devoting ten minutes daily to oral reading. Again, you must use a recorder to check how you sound. You may ask someone to listen to you read, but remember this exercise is intended to improve your volume level and not to create tension and prove you are a good reader. Therefore, read to someone only if you will not be criticized, but will be judged for volume control solely. Select an article from a newspaper or magazine, or read a letter or memo aloud. Try to change your volume, depending on the content of the material. Underline in blue those words or lines you wish to sound softer. Underline in red for louder projection. Play your recording back and determine if you actually followed your markings.

MATCH RATE TO MESSAGE

Will your message come across more clearly if you speed up or slow down? Should you speak slowly, evenly, rapidly, or with a varied pace? Think about the speed at which you talk.

Rate is related to the speed at which you produce individual sounds, words, phrases, and sentences. The normal speaking rate for most speakers is 120 to 150 words per minute.

As a rule of thumb, it would be safe to state that using any one set rate for all types of statements will win you no points. Apply the following formula. Match the rate to the thought you want to get across. To add interest and emphasis, you must decide which points are priority items.

Let's apply the above to a specific statement. You are talking to your boss and say, "I have a new, exciting project to present for your consideration." Which words are most important? How can you use rate changes that will help your message get across? In analyzing the sentence, you will readily see that the aim of the statement is to get your boss to listen to an explanation of your new project. Time is of the essence; there is not a moment to waste in getting the listener's attention. On the other hand, you do not want to risk being so fast that the basic concept (new, exciting project) is lost. Therefore, you want to use a varied rate, delivering the short message on two breaths at the most. Did you decide that the most important words are: I; new, exciting project; your consideration? Try saying the sentence aloud now, thinking of a rapid rate, but slowing down on the words I have isolated. You should be saying, "I (firmly) have a NEW, EXCITING PROJECT (*hitting each word individually*) to present for YOUR CONSIDERATION." Remember your aim is to get attention and encourage continued communication. You want to gain an active response.

Verbal suicide is committed by people who talk so slowly that the listener either goes to sleep or stops listening. The eyes are open, but the ears are not. The listener now begins to dream or think of personal concerns. A sure way to lose an audience is to use a plodding delivery that suggests you are either dull or ill. Right or wrong, we tend to assume that a slow, faltering talker is a slow thinker.

Taking this one step further, ask yourself how you evaluate someone who moves and acts slowly. Do you assume that the person who moves and functions with some speed is the one more likely to get the job done faster? It is conceivable that a judgment about how quickly you will perform a task may be based on how rapidly or slowly you speak. The opposite extreme—rapidity and nonstop talk—can also work against you. Your receiver may decide that you cannot be trusted with an involved job because you would not slow down long enough to attend to details. Your rapid-fire delivery could, of course, signal that you have lots of energy. The problem is that you exhaust your listener when you talk very fast, resulting in inattention because it becomes tedious to keep up with you.

Your rate should convey the idea that you are alive and well, that you are able to take on responsibility and complete an assignment that requires thought and action. The speed with which you speak should show consideration for the person to whom you are communicating.

Try to read both verbal and nonverbal feedback to determine if you are speaking too fast or too slowly. Is your listener looking at you or away from you as you speak? The pace you use should command attention and hold another's interest. Does your receiver look bored? Are you frequently asked to slow down or hurry up and get to the point? Are you out of breath? Do you sometimes talk so rapidly that your mind runs ahead of your ability to say the words and you forget where you have been and where you are going?

Pace yourself for your own comfort as well as that of your audience.

If you appear to be ill at ease—breathless and flustered—your interviewer, boss, or co-worker will sense your discomfort. It will reflect poorly on your competence. You will lose credibility if your rate distracts from the ideas you wish to convey. Deliver your information in such a way that your listener believes you know who you are and what you can do.

The rhythm of your speech will speak loudly for or against you. Make the words say, "I have a relevant message for you. I have the stamina and willpower to get this job done well."

USE PAUSES TO REFRESH OR IMPRESS

You can use silence to let your receiver catch his breath. Pause at strategic points. The pause allows you, the speaker, to organize and reorganize your thoughts, to catch your breath, and to read feedback. It lets your listener digest what you have said and gives the opportunity to supply feedback without interrupting you improperly. Do not be afraid to pause. Use the pause knowingly, however, and do not allow it to become so lengthy that you appear to have lost your way.

A dramatic pause is highly effective to emphasize a major point. It is most useful when you wish to impress your listener(s) with a new or different idea. It would be appropriate to pause dramatically before announcing a new appointment or a new goal to be set for the department. You might say, "In 1979, our department achieved a record by sales equaling $600,000. In 1980, we increased our sales to $800,000. Now, in 1981, I ask you to meet the challenge of—*pause*—one million dollars!" Your pause must be justified by the words that follow. "Our new manager is—*pause*—Joan O'Connor." Too many so-called dramatic pauses lose their effect. The novelty of its appearance is what makes such a pause powerful enough to hold your audience. Too much of a good thing seldom works in your favor.

Are you afraid to pause? You may think it is a sign of weakness to pause. You feel that everyone will assume you are at a loss for words. For the moment, it may indeed be true, but it is wiser to stop long enough to find the right word than to plunge full steam ahead and regret having said what you did.

All of us have the ability to think three times faster than we speak. Therefore, you can learn to present your ideas with greater fluency. Do not fill in thinking pauses with *Uh, um, O.K., you know*.

The phrasing you use and the rhythm of your speech should help you highlight specific thoughts and allow you to stress those ideas that require an extra moment to sink in. Know what you want to say and then match the rate to your message.

Read a paragraph aloud from a magazine or newspaper article. Pretend you are reading to someone else or practice this assignment with someone. Record your reading and discussion about the subject. Then take the quiz below. It will help you decide if you must change your rate. Base your answers on the playback of your recording.

1. Do I speak too quickly for most people to follow easily?
2. Do I tend to clip my words?
3. Are some of my sounds and words indistinct because of my rapid rate?

4. Do I sound breathy?
5. Do I speak so slowly that I lose my audience?
6. Are my vowel sounds dragged out to cause distortion?
7. Are my vowel sounds insufficiently prolonged?
8. Do I fail to get across an idea because I speak without emphasis and pauses?
9. Do I speak with phrasing that is comfortable and meaningful?
10. Do I distract my listener by saying "uh" while I grope for words?
11. Does the rate of my message add to my credibility?
12. Do I vary my rate adequately to correspond to my message?

A *yes* response on any but numbers 9, 11, and 12 will indicate that you should work on developing a more effective rate. Record yourself as I have indicated and read, speak, and play back until you like the way you sound. Use the sentences at the end of Chapter 6 to practice implementing rate changes.

9 SAYING WHAT YOU MEAN

SAYING what you mean will help get the job done the first time. Understanding what people around you are talking about will help you think and act with positive results. This means that you must use words that others will readily accept and understand. You should be aware of the vocabulary of the field in which you are job-hunting: many businesses and professions have developed their own language or jargon.

The data-processing field, for example, has a language that may work for or against you if you are involved in the computer world. On the plus side, you can speak to your co-workers with ease if each of you is familiar with the terminology. The negative aspect is the tendency to forget how to speak the language of your "user." The word "user" is the term for the client, whether it be an individual or a department, that uses the data-processing department. Systems analysts, programmers, computer operators may lose facility with English because they are working with machines, symbols, and feedback relevant to their world of work but not to the environment outside. Some individuals have told me they feel uncomfortable in two specific areas: making small talk, and explaining computer services to people in their company. It is essential to remain articulate in your own field, as well as in the world around you.

WORDS MEAN DIFFERENT THINGS TO DIFFERENT PEOPLE

Here is a real-life situation that may be familiar to you.

Ted, a man in his early thirties, presented a talk entitled "First Impressions" as an assignment to a class I was conducting at a national insurance company. The group, all middle and upper management-level personnel, was concentrating on improving presentation skills and, therefore, a question and answer period followed each speaker's prepared talk. The first question Ted was asked was "What is your opinion on the latest concept of image-making?" He quickly responded, "Oh, I don't believe anyone should present an image because that will work against one's being relaxed. You're anxious enough to do well in business and would want to be sincere and relaxed at all times without worrying about making an image. Creating an image would take away from the real self." Jeannette, who had asked the question, was in the same training department as Ted; therefore, it might be assumed that they had similar backgrounds and familiarity with the vocabulary of their work. However, Jeannette countered Ted with "But the impression we make is the image we present. It's how we talk, walk, and dress that creates an image." Ted smiled and suggested, "You have an interesting point. I'd always thought of the word *image* as something phony or false, so image-making struck me in a negative sense." The two continued to discuss the words *impression* and *image* as possibly synonymous terms. After a few moments, Ted announced, "I'll buy that."

Most people do not analyze and clarify what they say. It is difficult if not impossible to be aware of misunderstandings. These two individuals were fortunate that the circumstances allowed for developing understanding that led to a meeting of minds.

Often we are unaware of the one word that has "hit" our receiver in the wrong way. Sometimes, of course, your receiver's feedback signals trouble. You see a questioning or troubled look on his or her face, and you realize that what you are thinking and saying may not be what the other person is hearing and understanding. When you observe negative feedback, consider the verbal or nonverbal response as an SOS. Take the time, right then and there, to ask if you have been clear. Restate your idea in words other than those that created the misunderstanding.

Unanswered Questions: Misconceptions and Misunderstandings

How many times have you asked a question that went unanswered?

How many times have you made what you thought was a simple statement but which created confusion rather than understanding?

Few people are understood all the time by all their acquaintances. What can you do to cut down on unanswered questions and confusing statements?

- Use your mind and body to advantage. Your brain receives and transmits messages to the different parts of your body in order to respond appropriately in the complex process of communication. This means that you are simultaneously thinking, speaking, and listening while someone else is behaving simi-

larly. Remember that the other person needs to hear you clearly and watch you attentively if your thoughts are to be received with accuracy and speed.
- Auditory cognition may be more important than the visual image. Think of a time you conjured up an image of a stranger you were talking to on the telephone. Were you surprised to discover that the person was quite different from the one you had imagined? In telephone conversations, unlike face-to-face encounters, you are relying solely on voice and words. Every sound will carry extra weight in getting your message across. Each word is more meaningful when only the sound of the word is being evaluated by the listener and no facial or body movement can help you convey your idea. Therefore, choose your words carefully.

As Shakespeare said, "There's the rub." The rub is the problem most of us have in not being able to predict with total surety how others will see and hear us. Since people come in all different sizes, shapes, colors, nationalities, religions, with varying abilities, personalities, backgrounds, and biases, it is small wonder that words often have different meanings for different people.
- *Denotative* or *connotative* meanings will affect your thinking. Words have dictionary meanings, or *denotative* meanings, as well as *connotative* meanings, which are based on frame of reference. You will recall that Ted and Jeannette had varying associations with the word "image." Each defined it in his own terms.

Consider the word *jogging*. With the current stress on running to stay fit, it is easy to assume that Tina, the new administrative assistant, thinks of her morning jog when her boss suggests, "Let's run with this new plan." Of course, Ms. Jones would also be expected to know the word *jog*, but Ms. Jones does not know that when she tells Tina to "run," Tina's puzzled expression results not from a lack of understanding of the new plan but rather from the use of the word *run*. Tina is thinking of her morning workout and wondering how they will "run with the new plan." Ms. Jones, reading the feedback, thinks that Tina does not like the new plan. Each has a different interpretation of the message, stemming from *connotative* meanings of one word. Does it sound farfetched? I assure you it is not.

List in fifteen minutes as many words as you can think of with meanings that vary depending on circumstances. I will help you get started.

Word	Meanings
freeze (verb)	1. place food in freezer
	2. stop payment of account
	3. become glued to spot
buy	1. purchase item
	2. accept idea

- Give and take is an essential in communication. When you are talking remind yourself that you are *exchanging* feelings and theories. Select words that will aid you in this give-and-take process of sending and receiving messages. You may not be able to make an impact on the federal postal system, but you certainly can improve on the delivery of your own messages.
- Business interchanges take place via written and oral means.

Written communication is the exchange of letters, reports, memos, bulletins, and newsletters.

Oral communication includes interviews, meetings (one-on-one or group), telephone conversations, job appraisals, casual encounters, and face-to-face chance meetings.

To talk your way to a better job, you must practice more effective communication in both spheres.

Attend to Visual and Auditory Cues

Start today to pay greater attention to what you see and what you hear. Decide that you will concentrate on reading feedback.

Feedback is the message returned to you in sound or action by your receiver. You say something and notice that your remark evokes a different response from the one you had expected. You see by the facial expression or comment made that several of your words have triggered (now there's a good example of a word with varied connotative meanings!) an unexpected reaction.

What should you do now? If you want to get your message across, you will have to rethink and reword your original question or statement. Remember that what you say may be meaningful to you, but may not make sense to the recipient.

In reacting to feedback, you may have to ask directly, "Have I made myself clear? Is there some point you would like me to explain further?" Try not to put the burden of understanding on the other person. Do not become accusatory: "You don't seem to understand me. Didn't you hear what I said?" Make conversation comfortable to enable you to have fruitful communication.

You have to practice split-second timing to react to gestures, tone of voice, facial expressions, or words. The more you practice looking and listening, the more attuned you will become to adjusting to feedback. In turn, you will be a better communicator and get the job you want.

10 MAKE YOUR WORDS COUNT

WORDS, words, everywhere, and not a word to use. Is that your problem?

Just as you may need a large bank account from which you can draw reserve funds, so you need an extensive vocabulary to make your words count. By the time you reach adulthood, you have developed a working knowledge of 30,000–60,000 words in your native tongue. It is difficult to build a vocabulary that size in a second or third language. If you are not satisfied with your reserve vocabulary, often finding yourself at a loss for words, here are some tips for you.

1. Increase your vocabulary by using a dictionary to discover new words.

2. Start a list of words you would like to incorporate into your everyday usage.

3. Attempt to use at least two new words daily in conversation.

4. Listen for new words that others use, and list them after checking their definitions.

5. Begin to use in conversation the words you have learned from others. Be sure the words apply to the thought and the situation.

6. Avoid using the same words over and over again. Try to replace commonplace terms with synonyms.

7. Look up the meaning of words you do not know when reading a book, magazine, newspaper, or report.

MAKE YOUR WORDS WORK—OPEN COMMUNICATION CHANNELS

Words can convey positive or negative meanings. To help establish easy, effective communication, talk in positive terms.

Do not say, "You don't have to come to the meeting" unless you really do not want the person there. Try instead, "We know how pressed for time you are and can understand if you won't get to the meeting." This second approach tells the person that you are willing to offer a graceful way out because you know she has been working with a deadline. You are expressing a sincere concern for your co-worker. This is a concrete way of making your words work for you and count for more.

If a receptionist greets you with "May I help you?" you should use a positive response of "I'm hoping you can" before you get into the details. You will be setting a stage for yourself, illustrating your desire for help while establishing a warmer climate.

TRY OPTIMISM NOT PESSIMISM

Why be pessimistic when you can achieve more by being optimistic? Choose nouns and verbs that will be received with a smile rather than a frown. If you are able to make someone smile with your message, then you will be remembered with pleasure—at the very least you will be remembered; and when you have later contact with that person, you will both recall a comfortable atmosphere.

Exact words are not always easy to remember, but a sentiment lingers. Apply the idea Charles Dickens had of words: "Words are the dress of thought."

USE, DON'T ABUSE WORDS

"You know" and "you see" have become abused expressions. Enough becomes more than enough when you continually repeat the same word, phrase, or expression. Try to stop yourself by asking family or friends to point out words that you tend to abuse.

A woman I know, who is very successful in her work because she is a stickler for details, cannot hold other people's attention. No one wants to talk with her for longer than two minutes. When she talks to a colleague, Joanne's repeated use of "at any rate" turns off any interest. You speak to her and wish you could use earplugs to deafen the sound of those three words. Are you guilty of the same habit?

TRITE, ALTHOUGH TRIED AND TRUE

It is strictly habit that leads you to rely on trite, worn-out phrases. As times change, so do words. Be alert to the passage of time and the use of terms that "date" you. In the late 1970s, you would have been "Right On!" using just that expression. You would have been speaking the language of the day if you called someone a "square," but these words have outlived their usage.

Just as there are fads in clothes, there are fads in words. Try to keep up with the times. Recognize that what is natural in a school setting could be wrong in the business world. "Hey, man!" may once have been the greeting of the day, but it is an example of another expression that has run its course, and would hardly work for you at a job interview.

BREVITY IS THE SOUL OF WIT

Choose your words for accuracy. Avoid verbosity. You are verbose when you use several words when fewer (perhaps even one) would do. You may be perceived as false or phony if you go on and on after your point has been made. If you are asked for an explanation, give it and stop. (Hamlet's mother is suspected of murder because "The lady doth protest too much. . . .")

Once you have said what you think will convey your idea, do not get carried away giving elaborate stories and explanations which will tire your listener. If you talk too much your audience may begin to question your credibility. Let your sincerity ring through your words.

ORGANIZE YOUR WORDS AND THOUGHTS

You may be wishing as you read this book that you had paid more attention to those grammar lessons. You probably have become increasingly aware of your grammatical errors or deficiencies as you need to write and speak more often for business purposes.

For some, the greatest problems are in writing letters or reports. For others, the concern about using proper grammar occurs when meeting new people, or in a new situation, or when "under pressure" and asked to give an opinion.

Most people tell me they become flustered when asked to "speak off the top of their head." The impromptu talk does not leave you time to plan your words and sentences. It is natural, then, for a novice to worry about using incomplete or run-on sentences. You may even worry about the verbs agreeing with the nouns.

Perhaps somewhere along the way, you have heard that nouns and verbs must agree with each other in number. You also have a dim recollection of being told that nouns take adjectives as modifiers and that adverbs modify verbs. Do you know these rules but not know how to apply them? Or are you among the many who know no rules?

My recommendations are to:

1. *Listen* to yourself talk to friends, family, and business acquaintances.

2. Tape record yourself talking to others, both face to face and in telephone conversations.

3. Play the tape back with the express purpose of judging how you use grammar. Listen to sentences carefully to check that there is a complete idea stated in a complete sentence.

4. Select someone you respect, who understands your concerns and is willing to listen to you speak. This person should be one who is well educated, speaks well, and knows grammar well enough to point out your mistakes.

5. Analyze how you sound in comparison to others. Listen more carefully to radio and television news commentators—especially anchor persons—to catch their style. Recognize the way their sentences flow. Notice the structure of their phrases. Try to follow their complete sentences.

Every idea you wish to get across must be stated in a sentence that has a subject and a verb. This is the bare minimum. You must use a verb which corresponds to the time (tense) you are discussing.

Let's assume you wish to relate a story about your past experiences. Your interviewer has asked you to explain how your school activities helped prepare you for a job. If you will be talking about events that have already taken place, you must use verbs in the past tense. Therefore, you would say, "My activity in the student government *gave* me a great opportunity to do some problem-solving. I also feel that I *benefited* from being on the basketball team because the team spirit *showed* me how to work well with others."

The above sentences demonstrate the correct use of the verbs. Note that the verbs that are in past tense, showing what has already taken place, are in italics. The phrase "I also feel" is in the present tense because this is an emotion that applies to right now.

Here is an example of the wrong way of expressing the same idea. "I took an active part in student government and play basketball too, so I learn about getting along with others, and found out how to solve problems." Using the words "I took" is a good beginning, but then there is a shift to the present tense for "play basketball" and "I learn." It is then back to the past with "found out." These switches in tense may cause your interviewer to wonder if you did or still do play basketball. You are confusing your listener, and the awkward sentence will not help you impress your interviewer with your ability to speak correctly.

To restate the wrong example correctly, the following changes should be made. "I *took* an active part in student government and *played* basketball too, so I *learned* about getting along well with others, and *found* out how to solve problems." Do you see the pattern of agreement in both thought and verb tense?

It is certainly an excellent idea to tell your interviewer that you work well with others, but the way you express yourself will also influence whether you get the job.

Here is another example to study. Which would you say?
1. All the people are planning to attend the next meeting.
2. All the people is planning to attend the next meeting.

All the people serves (all three words, that is) as the subject of the sentence. That would suggest many individuals and therefore requires a plural verb form. To understand this concept better, try to substitute the words *he* or *she* for *all the people*. Would that make sense? Obviously not. You would need to substitute the pronoun *they*. Thus, you could say, "*They are* planning to attend the meeting."

You should have selected the first sentence as the correct one. The verb that I have been analyzing is "to be." The conjugation of "to be" is as follows: I am, you are, he/she/it is, we are, they are.

Which of the following two sentences is correct?
1. How many of us is going?
2. How many of us are going?

The explanation for the first set of sentences applies to these two as well. *Many of us* refers to more than one. Your response to that question might be "We are going. There will be six of us." Sentence two is the correct one. *Many of us* requires the plural form "are" of the verb "to be."

Despite the fact that many people do make grammatical errors, there is really no excuse for the use of poor grammar. You are expected to use good grammar when answering a phone call, when responding to a question, when participating in a meeting, when being introduced to someone, or when giving a report. You are expected to write properly, too.

Test yourself on the following sentences for your ability to use adverbs and adjectives. Which sentences are correct?

1. He did good.
2. He did a good job.
3. Maria works well.
4. Jim dresses good.
5. I speak English well.

Sentences 2, 3, and 5 are correct.

If you have doubts about your ability to use correct grammar, purchase a grammar book, or borrow one from your local library. Do the exercises that you feel are the most challenging, and practice writing and speaking grammatically correct English. If you speak English as a second language, make a conscious effort to speak it more often and with more people who speak English well. Enroll in classes where you will have the opportunity to participate in class discussions.

Advanced degrees do not always ensure the use of correct sentence structure. Your education may be excellent in technical areas, but you must be able to express your knowledge with accuracy and clarity. Clear, grammatically correct sentences must become a natural part of your communication pattern.

ARE YOU LISTENING?

"DO you hear me? Weren't you listening? How many times do I have to repeat myself?"

Are these familiar phrases? If they are, then they are surely not music to your ears. If you have heard them once too often, you are apparently guilty of not listening. Or, are you the one who frequently asks these questions of others?

Even Sylvia Porter, well-known expert on money matters, has written on financial losses incurred from poor listening habits. She pointed out, in a 1979 article in the Washington *Star*, that a ten-dollar listening mistake by each of the 100 million workers in the United States would cost business one billion dollars. Quite a large sum, you are thinking. Yes, and you can help prevent this expensive error.

Research in the area of listening has repeatedly proven that the average person retains only half of what has been said during a ten-minute presentation. After a period of forty-eight hours, the understanding and recall on the part of the listener drop another 50 percent, leaving only a 25 percent level of comprehension and retention.

Corporate heads have become increasingly concerned over the problems produced by poor listening skills. Since business relies so heavily on communications, there is cause for alarm when any part of the communication process breaks down. If you tend to be a poor listener, you may be making mistakes in business matters. It may cost you your job.

Fortunately, you can improve your listening skills, just as you can improve your speaking skills. Rate yourself in the following quiz.

HOW DO YOU RATE AS A LISTENER?

1. Do you listen only when you are expecting to respond to a definite question?
2. Do you listen to the words and ideas with the aim of answering with an honest response?
3. Do you listen to other people's explanations of subjects on which you have already formed an opinion?
4. Do you listen carefully to learn new information?
5. Do you pay attention to someone discussing a subject in which you have no interest?
6. Do you try to make a mental or written note, if applicable and practical, of points which you think you would like to make at a later date?
7. Do you consider it your responsibility to be a good listener?
8. Do you give feedback via facial expressions to the speaker?
9. Do you frequently interrupt a speaker?
10. Do you avoid looking your speaker in the eye while he/she is trying to tell you something?
11. Do you attempt to respond verbally to the speaker and the message being sent?
12. Do you readily show your emotional response to a comment, even if you may be overreacting to a statement?
13. Do you judge the message by the look of the sender?
14. Do you judge the message by the sound (voice) of the sender?
15. Do you readily believe statements made by well-known personalities?

Give yourself two points for a *yes* answer to questions 2, 3, 4, 5, 6, 7, 8, 11. Score two points for a *no* answer to questions 1, 9, 10, 12, 13, 14, 15.

If you tally a top score of 30 points, then you are an uncommonly good listener who gives excellent feedback to those with whom you communicate. Congratulations and keep listening.

A score of 24 points or better, indicating the incorrect response to three of the questions, still puts you in the better-than-average range. Review the questions you responded to incorrectly and make the necessary changes in your listening pattern to become an active listener.

A score below 22 should tell you it is time to sharpen your listening skills. Review areas in which you must improve.

Hope for weak listeners is in strengthening skills!

For twenty years, communication specialists have turned to the research of Ralph Nichols, who established an excellent guide to listening. More recently, experts in the communication field have become concerned with what is called *active* or *critical listening*.

Three areas that influence you as a listener are:

A. The level of your listening
B. Your responsibilities as a listener
C. Common weaknesses of listeners

A. YOUR LEVEL OF LISTENING IS AFFECTED BY:
  1. Listening to answer a definite question
  2. Listening to a question with the express intention of responding to it
  3. Listening to form an opinion on a controversial subject
  4. Listening for new information or "news"
  5. Listening to an argument in order to answer it
  6. Listening to directions which you intend to follow
  7. Listening to information on a topic in which you are interested

B. YOUR RESPONSIBILITIES AS A LISTENER ARE:
  1. To encourage and motivate the speaker by sending verbal and visual responses to the speaker and the message
  2. To maintain comfortable eye contact with the speaker
  3. To indicate a sincere interest by appearing alert
  4. To keep your face expressive to transmit reactions
  5. To ask relevant questions at the appropriate time
  6. To avoid becoming overly emotional to the speaker and subject
  7. In short, to stop, look, and listen attentively to those around you

C. AVOID COMMON WEAKNESSES OF LISTENING BY:
  1. Trying not to "tune out" the person or topic that rubs you the wrong way
  2. Giving the speaker the opportunity to speak without interruptions
  3. Using an objective approach to give the other person the benefit of your doubts
  4. Recognizing your own willingness to admit to being a poor listener
  5. Taking notes to aid you in staying attentive

To get ahead in a career or to be perceived as someone who has the ability to get a job done, you must be a willing listener. Do not let a tendency to listen only when you think the material is useful to you to allow you to lose precious information. Develop the facility of looking at new, although potentially dull, data as having some possible future benefit for you.

What you hear today may serve you well next week or next month, maybe even next year. Information should be considered for application in the future as well as the present.

In one of my public workshops a man associated with an engineering firm questioned the value of his listening to other participants' "dull" talk on real estate investments. He was demonstrating the Now Syndrome—my name for thinking only of the here and now, and what was in it for him at that moment. During the question and answer session, it became evident that several of the listeners were storing this new knowledge for use at a later time in the purchase of their own homes or future personal investments in property or condominiums.

In that same group, at another point, one of the men sensed the group's inattention until he introduced an explanation of a small lever. He stated that his company manufactures the part which allows for adjustment of the height of a steering wheel. Suddenly all eyes were on Jeff. Everyone wanted to know more. Listening improved because the audience saw implications for them and their automobiles.

Some Listening Dos and Don'ts

1. Don't practice the Now Syndrome.
2. Don't assume there is nothing in it for you, just because the material is different from what you already know.
3. Do have an open mind.
4. Do develop a habit of taking notes as someone else speaks (unless that would be rude), particularly when listening to a lengthy presentation. This is especially applicable at technical meetings. The notes will help you retain the information because the writing serves as both positive reinforcement for learning and an aid in the recall of data you will need to use.
5. Do try to separate the dramatic appeal of the speaker from the information itself. You may tend to give credibility to one who seems to know how to put on a good show. Isolate the logical elements from the emotional ones in the talk.

In a political campaign, you probably find yourself listening more attentively to a movie or television personality who supports the candidate than you do to the candidate him/herself. Don't be waylaid and deceived by the glamour.

In this case, listen for the message, so that you can come up with an intelligent evaluation.

6. Do recognize the power of the look and sound of the speaker. Try to be equally influenced by the words as you are with the polished presentation. Concentrate on capturing the message.

7. Do be aware of the short listening span you may have. Increase your attention span by distinguishing the important from the less important points. Maintain good eye contact to help you concentrate on the talk.

8. Do listen to understand. Try to summarize and even rephrase in your own words what you believe has been stated. This will ensure greater understanding.

9. Do keep channels of communication open by avoiding undue negative responses, either verbal or visual ones. Be selective in what you respond to, keeping your feedback meaningful for the setting. Know with whom you are dealing. Are you in the midst of a power play? Use control in reacting to statements made by a subordinate that require no immediate response. By remaining receptive, the continued conversation may lead to clarification more readily than your anger or hasty reaction might do.

10. Do take the time to listen between the speaker's lines. You are capable of thinking three times faster than you are of producing speech. Thus, you have ample time to digest, summarize, and even evaluate what someone is saying to you.

Identify your weaknesses in listening. This will help you to replace poor habits with strengths to assist you in listening and talking your way to that better job.

12 MAKING EFFECTIVE PRESENTATIONS TO SMALL AND LARGE GROUPS

DO you feel traumatized by speaking in public?

Do you dread being called on to address a group?

Did you know that the number one fear is fear of speaking in public? Now you know that you are not alone.

When Ed McMahon says his nightly introduction, "And now... here's Johnny," no one wonders whether Mr. McMahon or Johnny Carson is nervous. Except, of course, for Ed and Johnny.

Yes, even stars and accomplished performers get nervous. It is natural to worry about how you are going to succeed even if you know you are well prepared. If you are primed for the situation and the talk, then you will be able to perform more effectively.

The advantage a seasoned speaker has over most businesspeople is experience. If you know your field and your job, you probably can explain your position and responsibilities to anyone at the luncheon table or over a cup of coffee. However, problems arise when you are asked "to speak," or to give a report.

Let us suppose you are told that you will be the spokesperson for your division at the next company meeting. You are the one who is going to be responsible for explaining new procedures in budgeting. Your first reaction is very likely "Hey, why me? Can't someone else do this?"

Sure, either Joe or Jane could give the report, but this is your big chance to show your stuff. After all, it was you who developed the scheme. Take the moment and use it to your advantage. Probably Joe and Jane are relieved that you are the one with the pressure and glad that they will not be on the spot. But, consider the pluses after you have made the excellent, "dynamic" presentation. You will get the credit! Then, Joe and Jane may wonder why they did not seize this golden opportunity to shine.

I present you with a new, positive way of approaching the opportunity to speak at a meeting. You can be in a position to discuss an area that you have researched, making you more expert and knowledgeable than most of those present. Use the moment to full advantage. Project your best image.

Approach speaking with a positive attitude. To put your best foot forward and your best voice and look across, start with *preparation* and continue with practice.

Prepare in Advance

Preparation for a talk means that you first establish your assignment and your objective and then gather your data. This is a case of applying Management by Objective (MBO). MBO, based on the concept of setting your objectives and outlining the steps you must follow to reach that goal, can be carried over to the design of a presentation.

The first step after you are asked to make the report is to determine the *subject* and *purpose* of the talk. You will need to rely on your own background and experience while you begin to *organize* the information that will fill any gaps in your current knowledge of the area. You will want to have all necessary materials at your fingertips to ensure that you have total know-how of the topic and thus feel well prepared.

Your own full understanding, together with your self-confidence, will serve as the all-important basis for conveying your information to your listeners.

KNOW YOUR AUDIENCE

The next step is to *analyze* who will be in your *audience*. You have to gear your statements to each listener's position in the company, his or her background, and the relationship of each of the individuals to you, your department, your company, and the subject under consideration.

Ask yourself:

1. Will you be speaking to members of your own department with whom you will feel comfortable, secure, or defensive?

2. Will several or most of the group be as familiar with the material as you are?

3. Will some of your audience be hearing this information for the first time?

4. Are there terms, technical items, or new concepts that will require lengthy explanations?

5. Will you be prepared with the backup to define the technical jargon and have examples to clarify your points?

6. Will some of the listeners be inclined positively or negatively to your talk because of their relationship to you or your relationship to them, or because of their age, sex, their cultural, religious or educational background?

7. Do you know how people will react to the responsibilities that may fall to them if your project goes through?

8. Will most of the people be interested in hearing your report or will they be anxious to get it over with?

Try to imagine yourself in the position of your listeners and decide upon what *you* would want to hear.

LENGTH OF TALK

How long should your presentation be? Always attempt to be brief and to the point. Unless you must make a lengthy presentation because of the nature of the material (for example, finance personnel generally need to explain detailed figures), or you are given an assignment to speak no less than a given number of minutes or hours, then brevity should be your byword. Get to your point and stay on target. Do not digress or elaborate on points that you know you have covered adequately.

Stick closely to your outline, so that you have an orderly development of the material and resist the temptation to overstay your welcome. You must move along for it is impossible to make up for lost time. You are approaching trouble when your group starts to squirm, shifts their weight, and/or begins to look sleepy. You are in grave trouble when people start looking at their watches or get up and leave. You must cover basic facts, giving support material and supplying specifics to prove your points, and establish your credibility. As you approach your conclusion, let your listeners know that this is the final point. Do not end, then add, "Oh, by the way, there is also ..." Listeners forget the salient facts if you add information after you have concluded. You upset the mental set of your audience if you do not stop at what appears to be the end.

KNOW YOUR SUBJECT

Keep in mind as you prepare that you are the expert. From the moment you occupy center stage, you will be regarded as the one with the most knowledge. If you have been good in your job, if you have been keeping up with things, if you have done all that is normally expected for this particular project, then you should have a positive frame of mind. The men and women listening to you will believe you if you seem to believe in yourself.

Credibility is the top and bottom line in communication. We all want to be on the winning team and we all like to associate with the winner. You will more likely win over your audience if you project yourself as an achiever—one who feels confident of one's self and position. Express your full interest, and your enthusiasm will be contagious. Others will believe you because you believe in yourself. You communicate credibility.

Competency will be proven by the ability you demonstrate to discuss your data with ease and fluency. It will result from having done the necessary preparation, ensuring that you have all the facts on hand. Demonstrable knowledge with backup material, visual aids, and possible handouts will aid you.

Capability to make the presentation will largely depend on how comfortable you are speaking to groups. You may have to spend as much time practicing the talk as you give to researching and writing it.

Practice makes perfect, the saying goes, but you need to have good material to practice. Assuming you have gathered all necessary information, and you know that your specific aim is to convince this particular group that your new procedure is the best one for the department, you must now organize your thoughts into an outline.

PREPARE AN OUTLINE

I would like to have ten dollars for every man or woman who has questioned the need for an outline. These are the same people who bemoaned their fate and poor performance, wishing, after the fact, that they had had the outline to help them move along accurately and fluently.

There seems to be an unconscious negativism to writing

an outline. Perhaps you associate it with school days and term papers, remembering a lot of time spent for little reward. I guarantee that your rewards will be greater in business. The outline that keeps you on target will help you accomplish your objective. It directs you in moving toward that final goal of convincing your listeners that you know what you are talking about. It will help you say, "You can trust me to come up with the right plan that we can implement to everyone's benefit."

Begin your outline with a clear statement, in writing, of what you hope your talk will accomplish. For example, you might write, "I want my department to understand this new procedure for budgeting, and to recognize that this is the best way to improve our department's accountability and image in the company." Judging by the stated objective, you would have a twenty- to forty-minute talk. Notice that the goal is twofold. There is a need to define and explain the new approach as well as to prove that this is a step in the right direction.

As trite as it may sound, you must start at the beginning. The *Introduction* of a talk must gain the attention of your listeners. It should serve to lead up to the important points of the issue. In the above example, you might cite a startling statistic to capture your listeners and whet their appetites for a solution to the problems of excessive expenditures. "How can we justify expenses of a quarter of a million dollars, if our department's sales do not surpass the million mark?" You would continue by assuring everyone that fortunately, this is not what you are up against, but that you could be in that muddle if procedures continue as they have been.

Following a quick overview of the status quo, explaining what your department practices have been, you would lead up to past and present difficulties in the budgeting procedures and indicate why a committee was established to explore new methods. At this time, you are into the *Body* of the talk. You would explain who served on the committee and the meetings that took place, and you would justify why the new plan or method was selected as the best and most feasible approach.

You must give specific facts and figures to support all statements, and clarify any obscure or complicated areas. You might consider using a visual aid to support your premises. It could be helpful to prepare a flow chart showing the progression of the identification of the problem, the selection of the task force, the meetings of the committee, and the date of the meeting at which you are now speaking. It could either be prepared in advance or be developed on an easel-type flip chart as you speak.

Here is a sample of an effective chronological chart.

BUDGETING PROCEDURE FOR DEPARTMENT ABC

December 3, 1980	Company controller questioned heavy department expenditures and accounting procedure.
December 14, 1980	Problem presented to department at weekly meeting. Task Force selected.
December–January	Task Force meetings held to research and resolve problem.
February 2, 1981	Report back to department to present solution.
February–March, 1981	Implement new procedure.
April 30, 1981	Evaluate implementation and determine need for changes (if any).

Notice how easily you are able to move from one major area to the next by using the dates and items indicated. The chart, as any visual aid should be, is merely there to assist you. *You* are the focal point of the presentation; your visual aid acts as a supplement by adding information and understanding. It is not intended as a substitute for you. If there is too much data on a chart, then the viewer of the material may stop listening to you and pay attention to the written aspect of your presentation.

GUIDELINES FOR VISUAL AIDS*

1. Determine, in advance, how your subject will be *enhanced* by the use of an aid.
2. Review subject matter to establish the *time* at which the aid will be most meaningful and beneficial.
3. Ascertain which *type* of aid will be most helpful in *reinforcing* the information to be presented.
4. Prepare or order aid, allowing ample time to *review* use of aid or to make adjustments, corrections, or changes.
5. *Practice* the presentation, using the aid as it will be employed.
6. *Arrange* for placement of aid, backup equipment, technical assistance as dictated by group requirements.

In selecting an aid, you should consider:

Clarity
Legibility
Brevity
Color
Appeal
Relevancy
Timeliness
Technical accuracy
Practicality
Aids should help not hinder
Aids should clarify not confuse
Aids should be attractive not distracting
Aids should work for you not against you
Aids should add to your effectiveness not subtract from credibility
Aids should inform not irritate
Aids should assist you not replace you
A good aid Adds Information Dynamically

*Copyright 1980 DynamiComm.

For variety, it is possible to use audiovisual aids, if it is appropriate and feasible. A cassette tape played back on a videorecorder might illustrate a group in action or show steps in a manufacturing process. Use only as much tape and time as are dictated by your needs and those of your audience.

Lengthy films, slide shows, or video replays may put your group to sleep or cause them to forget your role. At all cost, do not dim the lights so much that you end up in the dark, or that your audience begins to snooze. Keep yourself in the spotlight and remember you are still the essential ingredient, visually and audibly. Be sure to have an extra extension cord and an extra projector bulb in reserve.

Check on the placement of the podium or table from which you will be speaking. Try to place yourself centrally.

It is best to have the screen or easel within easy reach. A pointer, even a ruler or pen or marker, will make you appear more polished and professional. Stand about two feet from your aid and use a pointer. Be sure not to turn your back on the audience. Point to the board or chart, turn, and then continue speaking.

The size of your group and the size of the room will dictate the size of your visual aid. If you are in a large room and there will be a microphone, will the mike be portable? You will need to be heard as you move toward the screen or charts.

Suggested aids include:

Books	Maps
Bulletins	Miniatures
Cartoons	Models
Case studies	Movies
Cassette tapes	Outlines
Charts	Pamphlets
Circulars	People
Demonstrations	Photographs
Diagrams	Posters
Exhibits	Recordings
Films	Replicas
Filmstrips	Slides
Handouts	Videotapes
Magazines	Worksheets
Manuals	

The purposes of your talk are:

To Inform—which seeks understanding, reports, teaches, trains
To Stimulate—which reaffirms beliefs, pays tribute, appeals, entertains
To Convince—which seeks change and commitment, suggests solutions to problems
To Actuate—which directs behavior, supports and implements direct approach

INGREDIENTS OF AN EFFECTIVE VISUAL AID

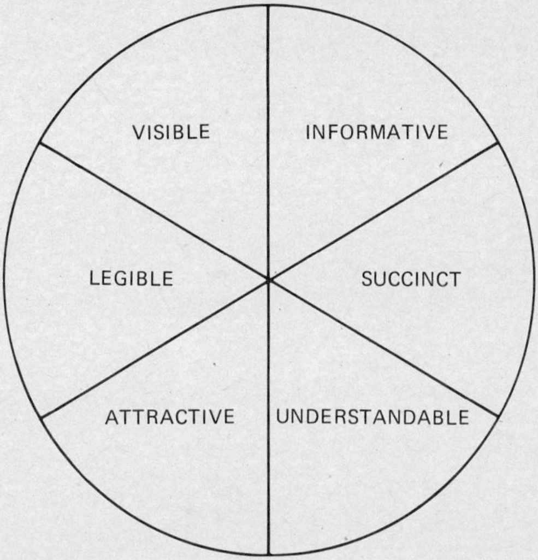
VISIBLE
INFORMATIVE
LEGIBLE
SUCCINCT
ATTRACTIVE
UNDERSTANDABLE

Methods of making a presentation include:

Impromptu	On the spot, off the cuff, unprepared. Drawn from background, as in impromptu report at meeting
Extemporaneous	Uses notes, some preparation time, drawing upon knowledge and experience, as in planned operating or technical report, sales appeal, welcome speech
Manuscript	Complete preparation of full text, reading word for word, as in annual report, acceptance speech, financial update
Memorized	Complete preparation of full text, memorizing all material, as in annual

report to board, acceptance speech, sales pitch, political address, media or press announcements

You may have thought you were giving an extemporaneous talk when you spoke with no preparation time, but you were really giving an impromptu talk. This is the most usual form of participation at general meetings.

Preparation with notes in outline or helter-skelter form leads to the extemporaneous speech given at weekly or monthly gatherings or departmental or interdepartmental meetings. It is the most appropriate for frequent get-togethers and for able businesspeople.

A manuscript should be written when precise words must be used in a speech presented to a specific group to ensure total comprehension with no misunderstandings. The greatest problem, however, is to learn how to read dynamically and effectively.

A manuscript is required for a speech that will be read aloud, rather than memorized. Actors and actresses memorize scripts. Politicians sometimes repeat their messages so frequently that the manuscript becomes memorized. Unless you are a practiced speaker, you work against yourself by attempting to memorize. The usual problem is that you have learned words by rote but you do not know the ideas and outline of your talk. This means that you continually repeat the words you have memorized so that your delivery may become stilted and meaningless. It is wise to learn how to read well so that you can present the manuscript effectively. If you must use a prepared text, remember it is an aid. You must still be the one who commands attention. Your papers should not distract your audience.

All papers, whether numerous or few, should be kept in a folder or on a clipboard. The individual sheets should be clipped together, with each page clearly marked in color at the top indicating the sequence. The numbers should stand out from the text. Slide the page to your left or right, rather than putting it at the bottom of your sheets. If you are seated at a table or if you have a reading stand, the sliding technique is excellent in showing where you have been and where you are going. This approach will be more difficult if you are holding a folder, but it can be perfected. Test it.

Do not staple sheets together or keep them clipped together once you begin speaking. They become quite unmanageable if they are secured.

Underline words, statements, and questions which you want to stress. Circle or star key words.

Use numbers or letters, marking them in different colors to help your eye catch the important points. The colors will serve to remind you of voice changes, as well as the need to include major items.

A must for all presentations is to follow the two Ps: *preparation* and *practice* are essential to control nervousness, cover your material, and achieve results. To convince you, I am including a sample outline for a talk. It is applicable to any type of talk and will help you understand how to develop your objectives(s) and move along to supporting points.

Preparation and *practice* will help you to reach the concluding portion of your presentation knowing you have done a complete job. The two Ps will also help you answer questions more effectively. (Read the section on responding to questions at interviews in Chapter 13 for more specifics.) Your Conclusion should not be a reiteration of all you have said before. The salient, most essential factors only should be restated to reinforce and make an impact on your listeners. A lengthy final statement seldom helps your cause because your audience may feel that you have embarked upon a new speech. Use the following formula: Introduction and Conclusion equal not more than 15 percent of total time, whereas the Body of your talk should be 85 percent.

Grab them at the start and leave a lasting, forceful impression at the end.

Use the evaluation forms that follow to determine your success.

EVALUATE HOW YOU TALK
Use a Scale of 1–5.

Judge your abilities to speak to one person, small groups (3–15 people), and large groups (15 or more people).
1 = weak
2 = poor
3 = adequate
4 = good
5 = excellent

	One-on-One	Small Group	Large Group
Clarity of subject			
Organization of ideas			
Accurate language			
Words			
Sentences			
Grammatical structure			
Adaption to Receivers			
Response to feedback			
Fielding questions			
Wrap-up of Subject			
1. Summarization			
2. Follow-up			
3. Implementation			

Copyright 1980 DynamiComm.

EVALUATION FORM

Evaluate your presentation using a scale of 1–5.
1 = weak or poor
2 = fair, needs improvement
3 = adequate or average
4 = good or acceptable for situation
5 = outstanding

Speech content   1 - 2 - 3 - 4 - 5
Subject matter   _____
Support material   _____
Language usage   _____
Organization   _____
   Introduction   _____
   Body   _____
   Conclusion   _____
Visual Aids   _____
Delivery   1 - 2 - 3 - 4 - 5
Articulation   _____
Eye Contact   _____
Poise   _____
Posture   _____
Dress   _____
Gestures   _____
Facial expressions   _____
Vocal variety   _____
   Rate   _____
   Quality   _____
   Pitch   _____
   Volume   _____

The following sample outline should be used as you prepare for a talk. Support materials include facts, figures, examples, comparisons, audiovisual aids, or any specific statements that help clarify and justify your points. Generalizations must be backed up by concrete support.

SAMPLE OUTLINE FOR TALK

General purpose: _____
Specific purpose. _____
_____
Central idea sentence: _____
_____
Introduction: Get attention. Establish rapport.

Transition to body:
Body:
  I. FIRST MAIN POINT
    A. Support
    B. Support
    C. Support
  II. SECOND MAIN POINT
    A. Support
    B. Support
    C. Support
  Conclusion: Summary. Wrap-up statements.

Study the guidelines that follow to improve your presentations.

GUIDELINES FOR EFFECTIVE COMMUNICATION

  I. Establish your message.
    A. Know *why* you want to talk about the subject.
    B. Determine *what* you hope to accomplish by speaking.
    C. Be certain you have gathered the necessary information (data).
  II. Understand your audience.
    A. Know *to whom* you will be speaking.
    B. Analyze their needs and interests in relation to yours.
    C. Direct your remarks to their level of understanding.
      1. Consider position, education, cultural and ethnic backgrounds, age, and sex.
      2. If you can ascertain information about your listeners in advance, take advantage of the knowledge gained.
  III. Project a dynamic image.
    A. Maintain an alert look.
      1. Concentrate on developing meaningful body language.
      2. Establish good eye contact.
      3. Your posture should reflect your interest in the subject.

  B. Use an expressive voice.
    1. Vary your pitch, rate, volume, and quality.
    2. Sound self-confident and interested in both your subject and your audience.
  C. Choose words that will be clear, relevant, and varied.
    1. Be sure you understand all terms you will be using.
    2. Use easily understood sentences.
    3. Develop a broad vocabulary to avoid becoming repetitious or hackneyed.
IV. Use an outline or notes.
  A. Concentrate on a strong, attention-getting introduction.
  B. Be certain your remarks flow from one idea to the next.
  C. Let your audience know you have finished with a clear, concise conclusion.

By Rosalie H. Smith, communications consultant. Copyright 1980 DynamiComm.

13 INTERVIEW IDEAS

THE English writer John Galsworthy once wrote, "One's eyes are what one is, one's mouth what one becomes." Many of Galsworthy's stories were of workers and bosses. This chapter is concerned with how you present yourself visually and vocally to that person in the seat of power: your employer-to-be.

There are books, articles, and courses designed to teach you interview techniques. Since we do not regularly practice being interviewed, you should take every opportunity to read about or study the interview scene. It would be naïve to write about getting a better job without including this very important topic.

Start with the moment you set up your interview, probably through an employment agency, via written correspondence, or by telephone. As soon as you know the time and date, you should start planning for that meeting.

Consider what arrangements you will need to make to be sure you can get to the interview easily and on time.

Consider finding out about the company and/or person who will be interviewing you.

Consider the questions you will be asked.

Consider the questions you will ask to gain knowledge about the company and/or position.

Consider the references you may be using.

Look Your Best

Looking one's best means different things to different people. For everyone, it should mean being clean and neat, and dressed appropriately for the position being applied for.

If you examine the interview setting realistically, you will realize that the visual impression may become the strongest one you will project. The outfit you wear and your personal grooming influence the receptionist or secretary who first meets you. In the long run, the creation of that first impression may determine whether or not you get the job. It is obvious that the interviewer will look you over as you enter the room. Hence, it is important that your clothes be clean, fresh-looking, and right for you at that time and in that place.

The color and style of the suit you are wearing can help you set the tone. Bright, garish colors detract from you because the dress or suit you are wearing commands the limelight. Wear colors generally considered conservative—blue, brown, tan, gray—if you want to set a businesslike mood. Be sure that your accessories match or blend with your outfit. Plan in advance so that you will have the necessary blue socks for the blue suit (for males), and the brown handbag to wear with the brown or camel suit (for females). Be sure that your shirt is clean and matches suitably, as should your tie. Unless you think ahead about the clothes you want to wear, you run the risk of spending the morning of the interview searching for a suit, tie, jacket, dress, blouse, panty hose, etc., that are clean and fit you.

Do not add extra pressures to the day by neglecting your clothing beforehand. So many people are on diets these days that I urge you to check that pair of pants or the skirt that you thought fit you one month ago, just to make sure that the extra five pounds you gained or lost will not make you look messy. Pants that are too tight will be not only uncomfortable but unattractive. You have enough to worry about without creating extra concern for yourself over whether the pants or skirt you want to wear went out of style two years ago.

Expect the interviewer to make a quick evaluation of the way you look. As you enter the room the interviewer will note if you fit into the company image and look the part of the job to be filled. Remember, you are not the one passing judgment on how well you come across that day; the interviewer is.

Your walk and your posture often tell how you feel about yourself. Be sure you wear comfortable shoes, allowing you to stand firmly on both feet and to walk naturally. Avoid new or tight shoes; don't experiment with a higher heel that day. Take the time to practice walking, sitting down, standing up, and walking into and out of rooms. Does your hand stick on doorknobs? Then practice turning handles on doors. Nothing is too silly to try if you want to be well prepared.

To Shake Hands or Not to? To Stand or to Sit?

When you are announced, walk into the room, look directly at the interviewer in order to exchange direct eye contact, but wait to be addressed. If the interviewer is standing to welcome you, then extend your hand for a *firm* handshake. If the interviewer remains seated at the desk, wait for him to offer his hand. Wait to be asked to be seated unless it appears after several moments that the interviewer will not ask you to sit. In that case, say, "May I take this chair?"

Once you are seated, do not immediately light a cigarette. In fact, it is ill-advised to smoke at all, especially in view of the growing nonsmoker constituency and the campaigns by the Heart Association and Cancer Society discouraging smoking. If the interviewer lights a cigarette, inviting you to smoke, you may judge for yourself if it is really necessary. You may feel that you will appear more relaxed (and you may, indeed, be more relaxed) if you smoke. The rule of thumb I am suggesting is: put off that smoke.

As you sit down, adjust your chair so that you can sit comfortably, moving your body with ease as you talk. Do not sit so far back in the chair that you are slumping. Keep both feet on the floor, preferably one foot in front of the other or crossed at the ankles. If necessary, move your chair to an angle that will allow for better eye contact between you and the interviewer. If there are several people present be sure you can look at each one without doing an about-face to some other person. Pushing your chair back a little sometimes improves the sight lines. Do not move the chair into a totally different location because it is most likely that the room has been set up to be most comfortable for the interviewer. Do not pull your chair too closely to the other individual, infringing upon that person's space or territory.

Everyone asks what to do with their hands when they are being interviewed. "Is it good or bad to gesture?" I have often been asked. It is helpful to carry a portfolio which allows you to have something to hold on to. You may keep it in your lap, holding it lightly. It will deter you from very tightly clasping your hands or from playing with a pen or pencil. Try to gesture, if the movement seems natural to you, to emphasize a point or to include the interviewer in your comment.

When gesturing in a seated position, move your arm from the elbow, not the wrist. Hand movements from the wrist appear to be idle, unsure gestures. Your gestures should be firm and serve to release tension and add to your message. Chapter 5 on body language deals with this area in more detail.

FOREWARNED IS FOREARMED

It is strongly recommended that you have background information about the company you are applying to. You will appear that much more sincere and alert if you can discuss the firm with some knowledge. If you can impress the interviewer with your interest in the company, it will be a plus for you.

In order to get information, you may have to do some research. Business magazines such as *Business Week*, *Fortune*, or *Forbes* may serve as valuable sources. The *Wall Street Journal* and most trade newspapers can also be helpful. One of the best ways to learn about a company is to speak with people it employs. Another method is to speak to people who work in the same industry. Request publicity material from the firm.

If you live in a small town you may find that your local newspaper has done feature articles on local businesses. Be brave and call the business editor of your local newspaper or call the Chamber of Commerce or Better Business Bureau to gain background material.

You might want to check the rating of the firm in the Standard & Poor's report or Moody's investment guide. Your public library should have all these source materials.

You may be fortunate enough to learn something about the person you will be seeing. Recent college graduates who have made the interview tour may be able to tell you enough about an interviewer's manner to help you prepare yourself. It is always advantageous to know if someone has specific likes and dislikes.

Think about the possibility of being interviewed by someone who is very conservative. You might want to tone down your speech; you would certainly not dress in an avant-garde outfit, appearing nonconformist and perhaps extreme.

The question of drinking at a luncheon meeting often comes up. Order a Perrier water with lime and err on the side of caution, rather than risk giving the impression that you need the drink. You will be able to think, act, and talk more clearly if you have a straight tomato juice, rather than a Bloody Mary.

PUNCTUALITY AND COURTESY ARE MUSTS

To acknowledge the seriousness of an interview, be sure to be on time. Establish your own concern and interest in the interview by arriving two to five minutes earlier than the scheduled appointment. You would seem overly anxious and too eager if you arrived a quarter of an hour or more before the appointment. On the other hand, do not be surprised if you must wait ten or fifteen minutes. If you happen to have another appointment following this one, then accept any apology for the delay by stating at the outset, "That's all right, although I do have a two-thirty appointment. I know your time is valuable and appreciate the interview."

When you are asked questions, remember the following:

- Respond only after you have taken a second to think, so that you may answer the question completely.
- If you are not certain you have understood the question, ask for clarification.
- Give specific answers to specific questions.
- Do not go into unnecessary details, but take advantage of the opportunity to strengthen your image.
- Try to appear confident without being too casual.
- Avoid bragging but be certain you state your strengths.
- Use a vocal quality and rate of delivery that give your interviewer the impression that you are in control of yourself. Refer

to Chapter 7 on voice to help you develop a sound of competency.
- Be prepared to discuss some aspects of your résumé.
- Prepare several statements, in advance, explaining why you want to be in this field or in that position, or why you feel you are particularly qualified. You should write out responses and rehearse them aloud in front of a mirror, so that the words become comfortable. Using a cassette recorder, tape yourself and play it back to evaluate how the answers will sound. Do not try to memorize words, but be sure to develop phrases and expressions that will help you get your ideas across clearly and easily.
- Be an attentive audience and an active listener. You can pick up clues about the office, the job, the responsibilities, by being a good listener. Refer to Chapter 11 to improve your listening habits.
- Avoid becoming defensive to probing questions. Learn how to project a smile in your voice and face. If a question happens to border on a personal area, simply say, "I prefer not to answer that question," but keep your tone agreeable. Certain points about marital status, religion, and age are not considered legitimate for the interview.

You may be asked to answer these typical questions: "Could you tell me about your strengths and weaknesses?" or "What are your strongest and weakest points?"

Answer with care. Talk about areas you feel confident in, being careful not to mention weaknesses that may eventually be used against selecting you.

For example, by saying, "I have just enrolled in a public speaking course because I want to improve my presentation skills," you will be demonstrating recognition of an area that needs improvement while showing that you are a person willing to work on that concern.

"What type of work do you like or dislike?"

Again, respond with caution. This is being asked to identify where you might be uncomfortable. However, if you answer too readily that you would not want to work in a certain department, then you leave the door open for a refusal on the grounds that you do not favor that kind or area of work.

"Would you object to working with a female manager?"

The same advice applies: you are being assessed on your prejudices or biases, as well as preferences.

"Whom may we call on as references for you?"

You may have listed references in your résumé and should refer back to those already mentioned. Avoid giving the name of anyone who has not already agreed to be used as a reference. Give the names of individuals who can be reached easily and will give positive feedback.

DON'T OVERSTAY YOUR WELCOME

Be alert for signs that the interviewer has covered all the areas he wants to. There is a time to be friendly and a time to say "*Au revoir.*" Learn to recognize when the interviewer is winding up the session. The types of comments and the voice will change. Once you have established your credentials and exchanged some information about the company as well as about yourself, then you may notice that the interviewer is trying to end the meeting by looking at his watch. A clear closing message is "It was good of you to come and we will be in touch."

It is at this point that you should get up, thank the interviewer, offer your hand if he does not extend his for a handshake, and leave.

The correct follow-up to an interview is a thank-you note. Your letter may make the difference when the decision is being made between you and someone who has similar credentials and abilities. This extra act of courtesy indicates that you are the type of person who follows through on a job.

All you need write in your note is "I am appreciative of

the time you took to grant me the interview, and enjoyed meeting with you. I hope that I shall be hearing from you with an affirmative response."

The letter should be sent directly to the interviewer. Make things easier for yourself by jotting down the name, company, and date on individual cards, so that you have a ready file of interviews and contact people. This will facilitate letters or phone calls you may have to make to the interviewer at a later date.

An interview is a face-to-face situation that gives you the opportunity to present yourself in a self-confident and businesslike manner. Take advantage of the moment. Remember that small and common courtesies go a long way. Address the person as Mr. Thompson or Mrs. Wells, not by first name. Say "Thank you" to the receptionist who may have ushered you into the office. The omission of these courtesies will work against you.

INTERVIEW DOS AND DON'TS

Do be prompt.
Do be prepared. Have your résumé on hand, even an extra copy. Know what you have included in the résumé.
Do establish and maintain wholesome eye contact.
Do use an alert, comfortable manner.
Do be appropriately dressed and well groomed.
Do state your ideas clearly.
Do establish your credibility.
Do speak loudly enough to be heard.
Do speak at a varied rate to match your ideas.
Do use positive words and statements.
Do reflect willingness and interest to cooperate.
Do demonstrate good listening habits.
Don't ramble or restate what you have already said.
Don't repeat words such as *like, you know, uh, O.K.*

Don't include ethnic, off-color, or religious jokes or comments.
Don't use poor grammar.
Don't stare at your interviewer.
Don't brag or seem conceited.
Don't overreact, becoming defensive and abrasive.
Don't raise your voice and shout.
Don't use unpleasant nervous habits.
Don't overstay your welcome.

14
EFFECTIVE COMMUNICATION SKILLS FOR WOMEN

STATISTICS and projections of the 1980s told the public that more than 50 percent of adult women were working, and that ever increasing numbers of women were entering the business world in nontraditional jobs. Women are now employed worldwide by the same companies that employ men, with the same performance standards.

The skills a man needs are the same ones a woman needs to succeed in her career. Communication skills, the focus of this book, are equally important to male and female competency and credibility. In that sense, a woman who wants to achieve results should be like the man who wants to be successful.

A question often asked me by men and women who do training in corporations is, "What communication skills do women need to get the first position and then move on to promotions?"

1. Women need strong, positive, effective ways of saying what they mean.
2. Women need to look as if they mean what they say.
3. Women need to project their competency, credibility, and capability to perform the job.
4. Women need to believe in themselves and in their ability to both do the job and be perceived by others as capable of doing the job.

Read this story and decide if it might apply to you.

Peg, a senior research chemist with an international corporation, enrolled in one of my classes at the Hartford Graduate Center because she felt she had reached an impasse. She told me that she was at a stalemate in her career. One year later, she wrote to me:

> Dear Rosalie:
>
> I want to tell you of the change that my career has taken, since I feel that you were responsible in part for my having had the courage to make such a change.
>
> You may remember that I took your "Oral Communications for Business and Industry" course about a year ago. At that time, I was extremely ill at ease when giving in-house presentations to very small groups of people. In your course, I learned how to express my ideas more effectively, and how to eradicate mannerisms and speech patterns that detract from the message. (I am still working on some particularly stubborn habits!)
>
> This gave me the confidence to accept a more challenging position (as a senior chemist) with S—— A——. We consult in electrochemistry and perform sophisticated research for government agencies. Our success depends on effective communication of our results and studies.
>
> I recently gave my first presentation to an international audience of approximately 150 at a meeting of the national society. I received many compliments on the talk, which was gratifying since it was my first technical presentation. Of course, it helped that I was presenting work that I had originated, knew well, and in which I had great pride.

The point (which I hope came through) is that you have to build on your strengths and overcome weaknesses. Identify what you can do. List what you are good at.
1. What are your talents?
2. What training and knowledge do you have?
3. What do you do to project a strong image?

Peg recognized that she was not making the most of her academic achievements, her knowledge and credentials. Until she took my course, she had allowed herself to remain in the background and had avoided opportunities that would have given her visibility and recognition. She really did not believe in herself enough to take some risks. Until she put in twenty-four hours of communication training she did not have faith in her own ability to stand up in front of a group. During her first presentation, before eleven participants, Peg's voice often fell to a whisper. Playback of the videotaping, along with my critiquing, gave Peg the motivation and direction she needed to change.

You, too, may need to develop a better awareness of yourself. You may need to work on improving your verbal and nonverbal language, as Peg did, to present an effective message.

CHOOSE YOUR ROLE

"Why can't a woman be more like a man?" Henry Higgins asked in George Bernard Shaw's *Pygmalion* (which became the popular musical *My Fair Lady*). It would be naïve to suggest that men and women must be alike, any more than you would expect all females to be alike or all males to be alike. Since we are all different, you have to look at the realities of the generations raised between 1940 and 1970, a period that stressed different roles for men and women, and sex stereotyping. If you grew up believing that females should be seen but not heard (like children), that girls are shy and timid, providers of tender, loving care, helpers not initiators, homemakers not businesswomen, weak not strong, subordinates but not leaders, then you are possibly a person who sounds and looks more passive than assertive.

Are there exceptions to the rule? Of course.

If the typical female of the first six decades of the twentieth century was expected to be a wife, mother, and homemaker, then it is logical to assume that emotionally and culturally that is the role that most women accepted. Now, if you are a woman, you may be reexamining your role as you become part of the work force.

If you want to be among the "movers" that Rosabeth Kantor, the well-recognized business sociologist, has identified as those in executive positions, then you must make the switch from the traditional role of the female as "doer" (also Ms. Kantor's term). You will have to think and act more assertively when you go for an interview or participate in your annual job appraisal.

The results of the 1980 census have shown that millions of women are heads of households, and that they are working to pay the bills and support themselves and their children. Women are not working to fill empty hours and to earn "pin money." Women need the same gainful employment men need. This is why women are now found in all ranks—blue-collar, white-collar, management, executive, professional.

Maybe a woman is more like a man than Henry Higgins or George Bernard Shaw believed. She is an educated, thinking, working, productive individual. As an individual, she needs skills to secure employment and promotion.

Does a Woman Have to Sound Like a Man?

A woman has to sound motivated and capable. Her voice must be heard and her message must convey credibility.

The male's lower pitch is generally to his advantage. Anatomically, our ears find a lower pitch more pleasing. The considerably higher pitch of most female voices may present an immediate disadvantage. Many people associate authority with a low pitch and, thus, a woman with a high-pitched voice has to work harder to prove herself a person of responsibility.

Even women find other women's high-pitched voices abrasive. There is, however, something that can be done to lower a woman's pitch, even though the female's vocal folds are structurally different from a male's. Most women can learn new vocal habits which will help them develop a lower pitch. And it will be worth the effort.

Examine the negative aspects of the individual who uses a high pitch. Since little girls speak in a higher pitch, the grown woman will also be perceived as childlike in sound, and she may possibly be considered childlike in action. Such a woman is projecting a hesitant, unsure quality, quivering or shaky tone, breathiness, and perhaps squeaky sound. She may be viewed as a complainer because of the "whining" quality of the louder, high-pitched voice. As the person who has a high pitch tries to increase volume, she often develops a shrill, strident voice, which is associated with being overly emotional. In short, this person is not taken seriously enough to give her a position of power. Women who recognize these characteristics as among their own voice habits should resolve to spend time lowering their pitch.

Exercises begin with those on breathing as described in Chapter 4. Then try the following, using a mirror and recorder:

1. Whisper, don't speak, the vowels: ah, ay, oh, I.
2. Look in the mirror to be sure you are opening your mouth as you whisper the sound. Your throat should feel totally relaxed before you try to repeat these three sounds aloud.
   - a. Swallow and yawn to relax your throat.
   - b. Roll your head to the side, back, side, and chest, letting it drop down on your back and neck. Notice how tension in the throat can be relieved through this technique.

3. Now, quietly voice: a) ah; b) ah, yes; c) ah, no. Record and play back to listen to your pitch. You should be hearing a fuller, richer quality, as well as a lower pitch.

4. Now try: a) ay; b) say hello; c) say yes; d) say no.

5. Record and play back before you go on to say: a) I; b) hi; c) bye. Gradually try to become louder, but stop if you feel any tension in your throat. The high pitch is definitely the result of poor habits resulting from poor breath support and tension.

6. Add the sounds: ee, u. Pucker your lips for *u*, as in *do*. Spread your lips into an easy smile as you say *ee* as in *be* and *key*. Do not be in a rush to add words or other sounds. Repeat this exercise until you like what you hear and can reproduce the lower pitch without thinking about it too diligently.

7. Spend a minimum of fifteen minutes on the above, along with breathing and relaxation exercises. Do not abuse your vocal folds; stop if you feel tightness in your throat or tension in your forehead, neck, or the back of your head. Be sure that you are producing a clear, oral tone, not a nasal sound. Only on *m*, *n*, and *ng* should any air be emitted from the nose. Nasality is frequently a problem for women with high-pitched voices.

SHOULD A WOMAN GESTURE LIKE A MAN?

Strong gestures are, interestingly enough, much the same for a man and woman. A firm handshake is an essential movement to set the tone of a meeting or to close an interview with assurance. It is a positive gesture.

If you are a woman, you will not be thought less of if you practice the positive gestures to indicate that you are an alert, assertive being.

Use your whole hand, not just one or two fingers, when motioning and pointing to someone or something. Keep the fingers close together. Do not wave your fingers or hands aimlessly. Your gestures must seem to make sense or your body language will confuse the people you talk to.

Your whole body should communicate an image of one who is in control of herself, if not in command of the group. Hold your head up, facing your listeners, allowing for firm, direct eye contact. You show strength by a willingness to look someone in the eye. Shy, demure, downcast eyes work against projecting a competent image.

Walk firmly on both feet. Do not tiptoe, but decide where you are headed and move briskly to the chair, for example. Take your place and sit solidly in the seat.

Sit in a position that facilitates turning your body to look in the direction of the speaker, or moving as others speak to you.

Whether male or female, you will look insecure if your shoulders are hunched over and your head drops down onto your chest.

Face up to the person and the situation. Do not be like an ostrich. By burying your head in the sand, you will look fearful and will not communicate your ideas.

Practice moving your arms from the shoulder. Standing in front of a mirror, in the privacy of your own room, try to gesture with your full arm. If you hold your elbows very tightly to your body, your movements will be awkward. There should be a fluid look to your gestures.

Wear comfortable shoes so that you can stand on both feet. Do not try a balancing act, shifting weight from one foot to the other, or crossing one foot in front of the other. In a seated position you may cross your legs, but avoid winding one leg around the other. It is a common pose, odd as it may sound.

A woman should be sure that her panty hose have no runs or wrinkles, so that she may feel confident about the look of her legs. A slightly longer skirt can also make a woman more relaxed if she thinks others will look at her legs.

You should always assume a relaxed, but alert posture.

Look as if you are comfortable with your role in the meeting or interview. Do not sit poised on the edge of the chair, ready to be dismissed at a moment's notice. Do not slump down to give the impression (like the ostrich) that you would like to escape from the situation. Try not to clutch your handbag or briefcase like a security blanket.

Many people, women in particular, keep touching their jewelry. Do you frequently turn your bracelet or ring and twist it around your wrist or finger? Do you continually touch your necklace, earrings, pins, or cuff links, as if to check that they are still there? Try to stop these distracting practices as they tend to indicate insecurity. Practice holding your hands in your lap or resting one hand on the arm of a chair. Stop yourself from idle, nervous hand twisting or playing with a pen, pencil, or ring. These mannerisms are irritating to others and do not really help you gain control of yourself.

Women are encouraged to wear their hair in an attractive style that will not require them frequently to brush strands of hair from their face. Do not adopt a hairstyle that covers your eyes, as it will be a hindrance to establishing good, firm eye contact.

Be more attuned to how you carry yourself. Chapter 13 on interview skills has information on dress for business. The explanation of passive, assertive, and aggressive behavior in Chapter 2 will also steer you in the right direction.

Every part of a woman should project the "fair lady" image that she wishes for herself. Do not be afraid to be yourself, but do make the changes that will bring you a more interesting career.

15 I SHALL BECAUSE I WANT TO

READ the following success stories and decide how my approaches can work for you.

A thirty-eight-year-old woman in a managerial position with an international hotel chain, telephoned to ask my advice. "My boss tells me I don't seem to know how I sound. He thinks I'm annoyed or angry, but I keep telling him I'm not. What's your opinion?" After a brief conversation, I suggested to Judith that she attend a seminar on interpersonal communication skills that I would be teaching the following month. It was particularly suited to her needs because the class was designed for women executives. Following the session, we reviewed a plan to meet Judith's objective of changing her "sound." The video playback and my comments clarified for her what made others hear her differently from the way she heard herself. With hard work, and a little bit of luck, Judith reached her goal of presenting a positive, effective, nonabrasive image by making significant changes in the tone of her voice, matching her words and sound quality to the message she wanted to get across.

In 1980, I was part of an evaluation team for a manufacturing corporation's in-house management development program. One of the observers turned to me after a presentation and said, "Isn't it amazing that the last young man, John, seemed so smooth, so confident that I can't recall exactly what he said, but I have the distinct impression that he knows what he's talking about. Is it possible that the way he said whatever it was made me believe he has something to offer?" "Yes," I answered. "It's possible."

The method of delivery can change the message for the receiver. Twelve men were enrolled in this training week and each made a distinct impression on the observers, who would be giving appraisals that would influence the participants' progress in the company. This particular observer was evidently swayed by the strength John was able to project. John was noted as a strong candidate for promotion because he exhibited confidence. John did not know the material as well as some of the other men, but he showed positive traits with potential leadership qualities. This serves as a good example of how one man talked his way to a better job.

Moving Up the Ladder Takes Perseverance

It might be the old adage "Nothing succeeds like success." Then again, there is the cliché "If at first you don't succeed, try, try again." There is also "Practice makes perfect."

The more opportunities you have to shine and to practice what you do well the more experienced and comfortable you will become in the process. Stop periodically to evaluate where you are and where you want to go, and to identify your strengths and weaknesses to determine future steps to ensure that fast track to success.

Eric Berne's book *What Do You Say After You Say Hello* describes the Berkeley Subjunctive, a common college "game": "I Would if I Could, but..." It is also a favorite of many husbands and wives who claim they would like to please their spouses but somehow cannot make those necessary changes. I am assuming that anyone who reads *How to Talk Your Way to a Better Job* can, wants to, and will work toward that end. Thus, in thinking "I shall because I want to," you will gain more than by moaning, "I would if I could but I can't." Think "I want to," not "I can't."

To project your credibility, you can make the effort to change your speech pattern, to change your voice, and to talk more confidently. Ultimately, you can achieve the goal that you set for yourself very much in the way you follow MBO—Management by Objective.

Which of the types that Rosabeth Kantor describes in her book *Men and Women of the Corporation* do you relate to? She writes of movers and stuck individuals, explaining that much of what we accomplish, whether we move forward or remain in the same position—stuck—is based on our own self-image. You must determine your own self-image and feel comfortable with who you are if you want to advance. Ask yourself, "Do I want to move up or move laterally? Do I want to take on more responsibility? Do I want power?"

Are you ready for the challenges that may be coming your way? What must you do to gear up for the communication challenges of tomorrow?

One of the participants in a seminar at the Hartford Graduate Center spoke with me about four months after the end of the sessions. Jim, a newly appointed vice-president of sales in a manufacturing company, said, "I'm discovering it's not only learning to talk your way to a better job that counts, but being able to talk well enough to hold on to that new spot."

This is a critical point. When we are promoted, we often

make increased demands of other people, assuming that when we reach the top we will be able to relax and stop proving ourselves. Then we reach that pinnacle and find that we still have to keep producing because there is always something or somebody one step up, above and beyond us.

In Jim's case, it is interesting to know that he had worked closely with people who knew him well. They had seen him show his mettle and prove that he could come up through the ranks. At the home office he had not thought twice of the image he was presenting because his co-workers understood him and knew that he was a competent, confident man. They accepted that he was right for the job. Suddenly, as a vice-president, Jim was traveling cross-country and meeting with people who had not seen him in action before. The pressure was on him to make a good first impression, for, as Jim said to me, it was what he said and looked like that would prove to the new board of directors that he should remain in his new position. His communication skills during a one-hour or one-day meeting would influence the powers that be and might make the difference in his career for future years.

Another interesting success story is of a woman in her thirties who worked her way up to become president of one of the largest advertising firms in a New England city. She told me that she knew she could do her job and everyone around her knew she could do the job, but somehow she felt she was getting negative feedback. She sensed that she did not look the part of president. Part of her solution was to enroll in my course called "Oral Communications for Business and Industry." The result was a complete change of image for Kay.

Here was a capable, bright, dynamic woman who dressed in an overly "preppy," careless, too casual style. She lacked the chic that her agency typified. Her image was inconsistent with the high-powered sophisticated "packages" she was selling to major firms, many of them Fortune 500 companies. After spending many hours in the course, accepting my critiques and viewing herself on videotape, Kay made the choice of developing a new image. She said it was "high time" she took herself in hand. When I checked back with her three years after the course ended, it was interesting to learn that the new look was now "old hat" and Kay felt it was time to update herself again. Soon after, she was recognized as a leading woman communicator in her community.

Moving Up

You may want to change jobs to gain exposure or visibility. If the overall direction of your varied jobs is upward, be sure to build alliances through the exchange of favors within the structure of the corporation. Through these means, more information can be gained about people in different departments. Frequent movement through jobs and locations can be one of the best ways, and sometimes the only way, to guarantee being noticed, particularly in a large organization. You might change jobs simply because the new spot will put you in line for further upward mobility.

Career progress is often associated with specific spots and positions, but no career path has been so well defined that you may count on moving upward unless the environment allows for upward mobility and promotions. Certain jobs are, in fact, dead ends merely because no one in that spot has previously been promoted to a better position.

Ingredients for Fast Tracking

Who are the people on the fast track to success? They are the ones who are liked by their colleagues and who are friendly to others in the company and call them by name, being sure to know personal details. These are the people included in meetings that others on the same level are not necessarily invited to.

Self-image is tied closely to career progress. Anyone interested in getting ahead has to be concerned with improving those skills that will help on the journey. You have to be willing to take on tasks that will give you exposure and to seek the knowledge needed to advance in your career. It is sometimes necessary to begin in sales, move to marketing and research, or work in human resources and development, before progressing to officer-level jobs.

To move ahead you must perceive yourself as ambitious. Be aware of the countless hours you must devote to the pursuit of your career objectives; be prepared to lose free time, time for family, friends, and hobbies. Short of becoming a "superperson" able to split moments, days, hours, and weeks into compartments for work, home, family, personal interests along with career interests, there is no easy road to achieving upward mobility.

Get ready to grab hold of whatever promising opportunities present themselves, whether you are male, female, white, black, American Indian, Hispanic, Oriental, or a member of any other group. You have to jump when opportunity knocks. Be a risk-taker.

And every step along the path, talk your way to a better job.

Use the self-evaluation forms, A and B, that follow to analyze your strengths and weaknesses as a communicator. Any item on which your response is sometimes, seldom, or never will indicate an area that needs attention. Even a "usually" response signals a need for improvement.

Try to be totally honest in judging yourself and refer back to how you viewed yourself before you began the book.

SELF-EVALUATION FORM A

Complete the questionnaire below to analyze your strengths and weaknesses as a communicator. Now that you understand the communication process and the skills you need to talk your way to a better job, you should be able to evaluate yourself objectively.

	Always	Usually	Sometimes	Seldom	Never
1. I talk distinctly and audibly.					
2. I assume a positive attitude.					
3. I present myself effectively both verbally and nonverbally					
4. I try to listen actively.					
5. I give meaningful feedback to others.					
6. I organize my thoughts before I respond to questions or issues.					
7. I try to understand the viewpoint of others.					
8. I express my convictions without defensiveness.					
9. I work well with others, even when they differ with me.					
10. I try to be cooperative rather than competitive.					
11. I adapt well to differing situations in a group.					

	Always	Usually	Sometimes	Seldom	Never
12. I focus on issues rather than personalities.					
13. I take the responsibility for my actions and responses.					

SELF-EVALUATION FORM B

Evaluate how you present information on a scale of 1–5: 1 = weak; 2 = poor; 3 = adequate; 4 = good; 5 = excellent.

	One-on-One	Small Group	Large Group
Presentation of Information			
1. Voice: rate			
pitch			
quality			
volume			
2. Articulation			
3. Pronunciation			
Eye Contact			
1. Direct appeal to receivers			
2. Use of notes			
Body Language			
1. Gestures			
2. Facial expressions			
3. Posture			
4. Grooming			
5. Dress			
Effective Use of Aids			

Add up each column separately.
Interpret your score as follows:
Less than 41 = Improvement needed.
42–52 = You're on the right track.
53–64 = You are O.K.
Above 65 = Excellent communication skills. You should already to talking your way to a better job.

CONCLUSION

The aim of my book has been to give each reader an understanding of how to develop abilities to talk his/her way to a better job. The explanation of the communication process, verbal and nonverbal images sent and received, skills in breathing as well as in articulating and formulating ideas for individual meetings or interviews with one or many people, examination of climates and barriers to listening and responding meaningfully to feedback, and analysis of voice patterns and individual styles, should have led to a desire if not a capability to *communicate effectively*.

If you have recognized your areas of strengths and replaced poor habits with new, positive ones, then you should be communicating:

Competency	What you say and how you say it should tell your future or present employer you are competent and able.

Organization	Whether you are preparing for an interview or talking about a job, project, or plan, you should be conveying a sense of organization.
Management skills	Even the individual seeking a first job must convey through words and deeds an ability to manage himself. For those wishing to achieve positions of managerial level, you must demonstrate skills to work with others, assume responsibilities, and delegate tasks.
Motivation	You can only be successful if you choose to be. How you look, act, talk, and work must say that you want to achieve, that you are a motivated person who sets goals and works toward them.
Understanding	Through a better understanding of yourself, you will be able to put your best foot forward. Your understanding of others must also be reflected in the way you communicate.
Needs	How you talk and what you say should tell your listeners that you are aware of their needs, as well as of your own. The company's needs must be recognized in relation to your own.
Interests	Pursue your own interests, identifying your preferences, so that you can best serve your company while you feel comfortable with your job and responsibilities. Let your interests be known.
Credibility	The way you talk, walk, listen, work and respond to others will communicate your credibility. You must know how to express your capabilities to be accepted as right for the job.
Abilities	What you possess to make you the candidate chosen for the position must be visible. Your ability to speak well, to make a good impression, to do the job

Talents   required must be readily understood by interviewers or co-workers. You will help prove your credibility by demonstrating specific abilities.

Talents   The areas in which you can excel should be easily recognized. Know your own talents so that you can use them to advantage in selling yourself or your product. Make the most of your unique skills and let your talents shine.

Effectiveness   Do the job. Do what is expected of you. Speak with clarity and accuracy. To be effective, as well as productive, you have to look and sound capable, informed and concerned. You must follow through and communicate that you know who you are and what you are doing.

COMMUNICATE EFFECTIVELY

- Competency
- Organization
- Management Skill
- Motivation
- Understanding
- Needs
- Interests
- Credibility
- Abilities
- Talents
- Effectiveness

Yes, you can communicate effectively!

Copyright 1980 DynamiComm

ABOUT THE AUTHOR

ROSALIE H. SMITH, President of DynamiComm Training and Consulting Services, based in Hartford, Connecticut, has served as communication specialist for fifteen years, offering her professional expertise and skills to over 1,000 corporate and individual clients seeking productive and effective solutions to the communication challenges of the business and professional world.

An accomplished speaker, holding a B.A. and M.A. in Speech and Drama from Brooklyn College, Ms. Smith designs and conducts training courses for international corporations, including Fortune 500 companies. An active member of the American Society for Training and Development, she runs workshops on Assertive and Effective Communications.

Presenting seminars throughout the United States, Ms. Smith also serves as Communication Consultant in special programs for management at the Hartford Graduate Center.